STILL STANDING

STILL STANDING

THE UNTOLD STORY OF MY FIGHT AGAINST GOSSIP, HATE, AND POLITICAL ATTACKS

CARRIE PREJEAN

Since 1947
REGNERY
PUBLISHING, INC.
An Eagle Publishing Company • Washington, DC
www.Regnery.com

Library of Congress Cataloging-in-Publication Data

Prejean, Carrie, 1987-
  Still standing / Carrie Prejean.
      p. cm.
  ISBN 978-1-59698-602-2
  1. Prejean, Carrie, 1987- 2.   Beauty contestants--United States--Biography. 3. Models (Persons)--United States--Biography. I. Title.
  HQ1220.U5P727 2009
  306.4'613--dc22

                         2009038555

Published in the United States by
Regnery Publishing, Inc.
One Massachusetts Avenue, NW
Washington, DC 20001

www.regnery.com

Published in association with the literary agency of Alive Communications, Inc., 7680 Goddard Street, Suite 200, Colorado Springs, Colorado 80920, www.alivecommunications.com.

Manufactured in the United States of America

10 9 8 7 6 5 4 3 2 1

Books are available in quantity for promotional or premium use. Write to Director of Special Sales, Regnery Publishing, Inc., One Massachusetts Avenue NW, Washington, DC 20001, for information on discounts and terms or call (202) 216-0600.

Distributed to the trade by:
Perseus Distribution
387 Park Avenue South
New York, NY 10016

I dedicate this book to my Lord and Savior.
To my family, Mom, Dad, Billy, and Chrissy,
I love you.

Contents

Sean Hannity

There's a reason why the very first amendment to our Constitution protects freedom of speech and religion—it's because our founding fathers held as their highest value that the people had the right to speak their minds on political issues, and that the federal government had no right to interfere in their freedom of religious practice. Because of their principles and foresight, America is home to a thriving free press that takes pride in upholding the first amendment rights of Americans to speak out on what they believe.

Unless a conservative is the one talking—especially a conservative woman.

Mainstream media contempt for conservative women transcends traditional lines of race, profession, religion, and background. Hillary

Clinton and Nancy Pelosi are lauded as pioneering female politicians while Michele Bachmann and Sarah Palin are called stupid and mocked for not cooking meals for their families. Katie Couric and Diane Sawyer are breaking the glass ceiling, while Ann Coulter and Michelle Malkin just need to shut up.

In this oppressive climate, Carrie Prejean has rapidly risen to national prominence because she *wouldn't* just shut up. When asked for her opinion, she gave it. She put her values, principles, and faith ahead of her ambition. Then, after she refused to say what our politically correct culture demanded she say, she lost the crown she had worked so hard to win. But she didn't apologize or back down. She kept her head high and kept speaking her beliefs, to me, to other hosts who interviewed her, to the people who fired her unfairly, and to the American people.

In the process, she discovered she wasn't alone. When she gave her controversial answer at the Miss USA pageant that night, she was speaking for millions of Americans who define marriage as it has always been defined: as between a man and a woman. She also spoke, as Miss California, for her state that had just voted to reject gay marriage.

Still Standing is the remarkable story of a great role model for young women to follow. Starting with her unlikely tomboy beginnings—the child of a broken home who grounded herself in her faith and competitive athletics, which carried over into a late-blooming interest to compete in beauty pageants—she takes readers through the journey that ended with all eyes on her, with time standing still, as a nation waited to hear her answer to an inappropriate, loaded, and politicized question.

Never wanting to become a political figure, she is one now—and while her beliefs are conservative beliefs, very similar to my own, what really distinguishes her in the public eye and in this book is her courage, her fortitude, and her stubborn conviction in affirming that in America we shouldn't have to be apologetic for speaking our beliefs, we shouldn't allow ourselves to be bullied by politically correct factions that want to silence all dissent and label it as "bigotry" (consigning the majority of Americans to the category of bigots). Carrie Prejean likes to talk about how her grandfather fought for our freedoms at the Battle of the Bulge. Carrie is fighting for them now on the home front. Her grandfather would be proud.

Carrie Prejean's *Still Standing* proves our country can still produce citizens with character, citizens who live up to the standards our founders embedded in the Constitution. Read this account of an unlikely patriot in a pageant gown—and take hope.

CHAPTER ONE

My Moment of Truth

"**N**ext, let's have California, Carrie Prejean."

I looked directly at Billy Bush, *Access Hollywood* star and host of the Miss USA 2009 pageant. I strode over to the center of the stage, trying to display ease and confidence.

Beneath the smile, however, my stomach churned with anxiety. When you're on stage like that, though the bright lights blur out the crowd, you're in a proverbial fish bowl: all eyes are on you. The lights make you want to squint, but you try to smile and walk across the stage naturally, even though you've practiced this same walk ten thousand times before.

This was my last test. We were down to five semi-finalists. One of us would be crowned Miss USA. Answering any question before a world audience of seven million people is going to be hard; mine would be a lot harder than I could have imagined.

I stepped forward and reached into a glass bowl and removed the folded card that would reveal the identity of my questioner. It was Judge Number Eight—Perez Hilton, self-styled celebrity blogger and professional gossip.

"Are we worried?" asked the co-host, actress Nadine Velazquez.

"You should be," a deep voice said into a microphone.

I turned to face Perez Hilton, a jowly, boyish-looking man with blond highlights in his hair. It was his deep voice that had given me this warning—no doubt half in jest, but half menacingly too.

He asked his question: "Vermont recently became the fourth state to legalize same-sex marriage. Do you think every state should follow suit? Why or why not?"

It was as though I could feel time slowing down; as if silence was screaming in my ears, like tinnitus; I had to break that silence with my answer—and I had to do it now, before the silence grew and grew and crippled me, making me look hesitant or confused. I have never felt more exposed, alone, and vulnerable in my life. But I smiled my broadest smile and prepared to answer.

I was being dared—in front of the entire world—to give a candid answer to a serious question. I knew if I told the truth, I would lose all that I was competing for: the crown, the luxury apartment in New York City, the large salary—everything that went with the Miss USA title. I also knew, or suspected, that I was the front-runner, and if I gritted my teeth and gave the politically correct answer, I could be Miss USA.

For the contestants, the Miss USA event you see on television comes at the end of three very strange weeks. We had all been living together, fifty-one beautiful women from across the country packed into the Planet Hollywood Resort and Casino in Las Vegas, with a tight schedule of press interviews, charity events, and photo shoots. It was a time of intense competition, mental exhaustion, and, at the end of each day as we lay our heads down on our pillows, sweet dreams of golden futures. Everything was on the line for us—or so it seemed at the time. As those three weeks wound down, the number of contestants narrowed to fifteen.

I was one of those fifteen.

On the evening of the competition, on live national television, the final fifteen came down to ten.

I made the final ten.

And then, with my sister, my proud parents, my aunts and uncles and friends watching, they came down to the final five. I was one of them. I had survived the interview, the swimsuit competition, and the evening gown competition. There was just one more event to go. To me, this last event was the easiest. After all my preparation, I knew I could do this. I just had to be myself.

Suddenly, it hit me that the long months of planning, dieting, exercising, and practicing were on the verge of paying off. If I won, I would become Miss USA, headed for the 58th Miss Universe Pageant in Nassau, Bahamas. I would be America's girl at the most popular and most-watched beauty pageant in the world.

Even if I only won Miss USA, it would be a platform for national exposure. It would help me land my dream job as an on-air sports journalist on a national network. But even if I looked confident as I walked toward my goal across that stage, inside I was thinking: *What if I trip over my heels* (as several contestants had done in other pageants) *or give a painfully inarticulate answer* (as had also happened and been immortalized on YouTube). This evening in Las Vegas was my chance to fall flat on my fanny in front of the whole world. I squared my shoulders. *Miss Universe, Carrie*, I told myself. *You got this.* I knew if I saw it, felt it, the dream could become reality.

Then came "the Question."

Many commentators have called me stupid for not having the political judgment to look down from that stage at Perez Hilton and give him the answer he so desperately wanted to hear.

Instead, I said:

> Well, I think it's great that Americans are able to choose one or the other. We live in a land that you can choose same-sex marriage or opposite marriage. And you know what, in my country, in my family, I think that I believe that marriage should be between a man and a woman, no offense to anybody out there. But that's how I was raised, and that's how I believe that it should be—between a man and a woman.

I could see Perez and the other judges slump back in their chairs, mouths gaping with disbelief. Perez's round school-boy face sagged—he looked absolutely devastated. Perez turned away from me, refusing to make eye contact.

It was as if I had just set off an atomic bomb. After a moment of stunned silence, everyone in the audience started talking. I heard cheers and boos; then the roar of hundreds of conversations drowned out everything else.

As I later told Matt Lauer on the *Today Show*, I knew immediately that I would lose the competition because of my answer, because I had spoken from my heart, from my beliefs, and for my God. I also spoke for the majority of the people of California, but not, I was sure, for the majority of the judges on the panel. They as a group represented the values of Hollywood; those aren't my values, and though I didn't want to offend anyone, it was more important to me to be biblically correct than politically correct.

It's a sad fact of life, but I knew political correctness was powerful enough to deny me the opportunity to be Miss USA. As painful as losing is, especially for a competitor like me, I could live with that—because the crown was not worth winning if it meant compromising my beliefs. What I didn't know was that merely for expressing a point of view identical to that of a majority of California voters, the President, and most Americans, I would be publicly labeled a bigot and a bitch, a Nazi, and a "c**t." I would be the victim of a succession of well-planned dirty tricks in which the same people who put me on an airplane to New York would then hold a press conference to bemoan the fact that I was not in Los Angeles, doing my job. I would have my personal medical information and emails publicly released without my knowledge or consent. I would have personal information from my past aired publicly, as if I were running for president. I would receive a televised death threat from a prominent British politician— and no one I worked with in the Miss California or Miss USA pageants would even bother to stand up to say a word in my defense. Within weeks I would be fired as Miss California in the worst possible way, getting the news from my interviewer, Billy Bush, while I was on his radio show.

The strange part is that I would learn that I—a 22-year-old beauty queen from San Diego—had dared to speak out and say what some of the most influential people in the country will only tell me in a whisper, that marriage should only be between a man and a woman.

What I went through told me something about America. There is something broken in our culture when a majority of Americans are afraid to speak out on a prominent issue. There is something sick about a political correctness smear machine that can be turned on instantly and can throw so much hatred at a young woman who dared to speak her mind.

What I went through also told me something about myself. An angry detractor told one of my defenders that I was "going to die broke, drunk, and lonely. We are going to destroy her. She doesn't know what she is up against." Would I do it again? As I told Matt Lauer, I gave my answer, and I wouldn't change it for the world. Ask me a specific question, and you will get a specific answer. I've never been one to turn down a dare, and I'm not about to back down from what I believe.

I went out on that stage knowing who I was. They threw everything they had at me—and it's still coming: the lies, the hate, and the personal attacks. But I don't think they knew who they were messing with. There are a lot of bullies in our culture—bullies who like to think that conservative women, Christians, and people who believe in traditional values are fair game; that we can be mocked and pilloried at will because they're cool and we're not; because they're worldly and we're prudes; because they command the cultural heights and look on normal, church-going Americans as dangerously bigoted and ignorant people who need to be reformed. As I've learned, the guardians of political correctness, the ones most likely to claim to worship tolerance, are the ones most utterly intolerant of disagreement.

But I have news for them: I came up the hard way, and I know how to deal with bullies; I'm still standing, and they're not going to take me down.

CHAPTER TWO

Standing Up for Myself

You might think of me as the kind of girl who lives for the sash and crown, a human Barbie doll who started as a child contestant, like the little girls you see on TLC's *Toddlers and Tiaras*, complete with the pushy mother, the fake eyelashes, and loads of make-up. In my few years in the pageant world, I did know some girls who were like that. I was never one of them.

I have always been fiercely independent and competitive. To tell the truth, I have always been, heart and soul, an athlete—a female "jock."

One other thing about me doesn't fit the beauty queen mold: I don't like people telling me what I can or cannot say. It all goes back to a day when I was eight years old, and my court-appointed lawyer sat me down and said, "You can't have your own voice."

I didn't like being told that at age eight, and I don't like it now.

I was brought up in Vista, a suburb north of San Diego. I might have been born and raised on "the Left Coast," but in cultural terms, I really come from the smack dab middle of America. You can ask a lot of Californians, and they'll tell you the same thing—that their California is the California of Ronald Reagan (our former governor), John Wayne (who has an airport named after him in Orange County), and church-going communities (from the Catholic missions of our past and present to some of the biggest and most notable Evangelical churches in America). This is especially true if they come from California's ranching and farming country, or the areas inland from the coast, or like me, from San Diego, which remains a Navy and Marine Corps town. Vista, where I grew up, is the kind of place where Veterans Day means something more than a day off work, and school prayer means something more than a moment of meditation. Take away the palm trees and Pacific breeze, and Vista could be in Texas, Iowa, or Georgia.

I was a quiet kid—a very quiet kid. As a toddler, I was the kind of kid parents could take to a restaurant without fear of embarrassment. I would just look around the room at all the people, completely observant of the scene and totally silent (though my mother jokes I am making up for my silence now). In fact, I didn't speak at all until I was four years old. That was just fine, however, because I had my sister, Christina, to speak for me. Chrissy, who is just eleven months older than I am, is practically my twin (except in one respect: she is every bit as liberal as I am conservative). My sister is also a source of tremendous pride for my mother, Francine, and my father, Will. Chrissy is today a second lieutenant in the United States Air Force, serving our country.

My older brother, Billy Arnone, showed me the value of independence, and how to survive by setting a goal and making it on your own. He has been riding dirt bikes since he was five years old, and is now a professional dirt bike rider, doing what he loves best. The media went after him when I came under fire, even labeling him as a racist (based solely on his appearance: short hair and tattoos). But Billy is a good guy and has always been very supportive of me. I never knew him well, since he is a good bit older than I am, but I have always loved and respected him. He is a strong, independent man who has been making it on his own since he was eighteen years old.

I especially remember my mother always being at home for us kids. She played a huge role in my upbringing, being a stay-at-home mom for over twenty years. Hers was literally a 24/7 job—picking us up from school, feeding us, clothing us, bathing us, and especially as we grew older spending time with us, listening to us, answering our questions, molding our characters. In fact, I never had a babysitter. While dad traveled, supporting our family, mom would stay with us. I owe so much to her.

I was also very much a daddy's girl. I would wait for him to come home from work at night and then run out to meet him. He read us bedtime stories whenever he was at home, and always encouraged us to say our prayers.

It was wonderful growing up in my family, side-by-side with my siblings. Chrissy in particular has been my best friend and soul sister. But we almost didn't grow up together at all.

When I was two years old, my parents went out shopping at the day-after New Year's sales, leaving Chrissy and me at home under my grandparents' supervision. I remember seeing a bunch of pink pills left out on the counter. I also remember Chrissy saying, "Sissy, look, they're candy, and they're your favorite color." She dared me to eat some. I went a step further, taking several bunches and swallowing them whole. Chrissy took some, but didn't like the taste and spat them out.

They were my grandfather's pills for his high blood pressure. And I had a stomach full of them.

Several hours later, after I had been put down for a nap, my grandmother tried—and failed—to wake me. Of course this frightened her, but she did not know what to do. Fortunately, an aunt of mine who had come by had the presence of mind to see that something was seriously wrong. She searched around the house, saw the pills on the floor, and called 911.

At the hospital, the physicians told my parents that after pumping my stomach, there was nothing else they could do. I was in a coma. There was, they said, no antidote for what I had taken. My parents, grandparents, cousins, distant relatives—the entire family came to the hospital. I remember Grandpa telling me he got on his knees, sobbing and asking God not to let me die. My parents prayed over me, begging the Lord to give me the chance to live. It was an emotional day for my family. But after twenty-four hours, I opened my eyes and slowly came out of the coma. As deeply traumatic as those days were for my parents, I was far too young to remember much about them.

But I do vividly remember the trauma at age eight that irrevocably shaped the rest of my life. For years, my parents had argued. I can't say their arguing bothered me much as a child, because they did it so often that I merely thought it was something that all married people did. Kids have their own defense mechanisms, and mine protected me to the point that I considered myself happy and my home normal. My parents' divorce changed all that. It set off a custody battle that went on for almost ten years. The irony of it was that we were practically grown when it was all over. It was a very ugly process, with harsh recriminations and charges thrown from one parent to the other. (Later, when I became a hate figure for the cultural left, my parents' divorce records were found and exploited as a way to try to embarrass me.)

Today, divorce might sound like a commonplace life event, and you might think it was especially common in California in the late 1980s and early 1990s; but in our community, divorce was rare. I had only one friend in school, Jennifer, whose parents had divorced. Jennifer and Chrissy were the only girls I knew who could relate to me, who knew what it was like to hear parents try to enlist their children to take sides, who knew what it was like to live in two homes, to have two closets and two beds, or two Christmases and two Thanksgivings every year.

This happened, as I tell my parents today, because they were being selfish. They do not disagree with me. The good news is that, however bitter and tragic their divorce, they've grown through it; they now get along just fine, and they have become tremendously loving and supportive parents. In fact, I couldn't have made it through the ordeal I faced as Miss California if I hadn't had my Mom and Dad by my side. And to be by me, they had to be by each other. But in my youth, it was a very different story. The divorce put distance between me and my parents, even as it intensified my relationship with my sister. I also had to grow up fast and learn to do things on my own.

I got a little unwanted kick in that direction from a judge. Caught between two wrangling parents, the court appointed an attorney for my sister and me to find out which parent we really wanted to live with—and which parent would actually be the best for us to live with. Looking back, perhaps I can see some logic behind the court's action. Still, it might have made more sense for the court to use a child psychiatrist or a family counselor to find out what living arrangement would be best for us.

But we were not assigned a child psychiatrist or a family counselor. The court appointed a lawyer—a harsh, aggressive woman—who would sit Chrissy and me in front of her desk in her downtown office while she paced around and discussed legal concepts in language no 8-year-old could possibly understand.

One thing did come through, however, loud and clear.

"You can't have your own voice," the lawyer said. "That's why you need to keep meeting with me once a week. Only then can I go to the court and speak for you." She would stare us down with her large, cold eyes, trying to silence us. Then the lawyer would engage us in long conversations meant to tease out some telling fact that would allow her to determine which parent should raise us.

At the end of it all, nothing was accomplished, except that all the money my parents would have spent on our college educations went into the hands of lawyers.

In the midst of all this complication and heartache, I was still a child. I yearned for structure. I needed a sense of belonging. I wanted a place to pour out all my frustration and work off all my sadness.

My sister and I found that place in sports.

My parents had put me in softball and basketball when I was little. I remember my love of sports began when I was five years old, watching my brother play all stars for little league baseball. Dad coached Billy, who was an amazing athlete. Seeing him play, I knew I wanted to be out there on the field some day. My sister and I were always running around, chasing foul balls. Softball became my life for a long time. When I was a freshman in high school, our team went on to win the national championship in Spokane, Washington. While I was still in middle school, however, I discovered that I had a new passion, one that was better suited to a tall girl like me: basketball.

During high school, I was a four-sport athlete—track (I ran cross country), one season on the women's golf team, more softball, but above all, basketball. I played guard/forward and soon became our team's leading three-point shooter. I was on the team for all four years of high school and started every game (and I've got the scars to prove it). I would eventually start looking at colleges where I could play.

Chrissy was also on my team. She had my back and I had hers. In one critical match against Fallbrook High School, she and I managed to win the game for Vista with five three-point shots. I was on fire that night. And it is still one of the best memories of my life. I proved to myself what I could do when I pursued a passion, body and soul.

I was active in student politics, as well. In my sophomore year, I ran for athletic chairperson and won. In my junior and senior year, I ran for associated student body president, and won again, both times. Apathy was not a problem for me—I liked being involved in school activities and being a leader, and I understood the value of keeping busy. High School is when a lot of kids start making bad decisions, and I was fortunate in being able to steer myself away from a lot of choices

I might later regret. Being so active in sports and leadership activities helped; so did my own desire to maintain a good reputation; and it didn't hurt to have a slightly older sister looking after me. Most of all, I had a strong foundation in my faith, especially through my involvement with Christian Club and Fellowship of Christian Athletes.

Even through the turmoil of their divorce, my parents had encouraged my Christian faith and kept me going to church. I had decided at a very early age to give my heart to Jesus, and he became my rock, quite literally my salvation. I went to a small church in Vista for most of my life, and while my relationship with Jesus deepened in high school, it blossomed even further when I was eighteen. At that time, some of my friends and I gravitated toward the ministry of a former defensive back for the San Diego Chargers, Miles McPherson, and his church, which he called The Rock. The first few times I attended, it was a humble ministry (at least compared to what it is today) meeting in Montezuma Hall at San Diego State. The church had 3,000 members, but relied on folding chairs for about a third of those who came, and at the end of the evening service, we had to stack all the chairs against the wall. I didn't meet Miles then, but he and his congregation, now one of the largest churches in San Diego, would eventually live up to their name for me, supporting me, standing up for me, being my rock, when the storm fell upon me later.

As a committed Christian, I cared a lot about my reputation as a leader in high school—not because I was worried about being cool or even being liked. I didn't want to be seen as that girl who said she was a Christian and then didn't act like one. I didn't want to be the hypocrite who went to church on Sunday, but got drunk or stoned on the weekend; who would hang out with the "cool" or popular crowd and try to capitalize on her youth and good looks; and who let herself be driven by peer pressure to do things she'd later regret. I didn't want this, because I knew that kind of behavior was not what Christ wanted me to model for my peers.

Some might have called me a prude, but I think most people got who I was. They respected me for my athleticism and for being solid in my identity. They knew I was dedicated to what I was doing and saw how organized I was. I was very cautious in choosing my friends. I dated, but my boyfriends were few. I didn't run with the popular "cool" crowd; I would hang out with my fellow athletes; but if I didn't seek to be the most popular girl on campus, I wasn't a loner either, and I had enough respect from my peers to be successful in student politics. Being president of the associated student body kept me focused on being organized, keeping up my grades, and acting as a role model to my fellow students. My lunches were often taken up with holding meetings.

Unlike my sister though, who was Student of the Year, excelling in academics *and* at sports, I wasn't so gifted when it came to academics. I got by with some Cs and a lot of Bs. But in one respect, we were exactly alike: Chrissy was never one to let people push her around or walk all over her.

I had another anchor in my early life, Frank Coppola, my grandfather.

After the divorce, Mom, Chrissy, and I moved from house to house. But we always lived close to my grandparents. At one point, we lived in a mobile home in the same mobile home park as my grandparents, and I saw a lot of Grandpa and Grandma.

Grandma still knows how to enjoy life. She is healthy and lively as ever at ninety. I remember when I was a little she would always be at home cooking for us. Grandma and Grandpa were married for sixty-four years. I always looked to their marriage as my model: long-lasting and filled with laughter.

Grandpa was a character, a mix of whimsical humor and "Old School" propriety.

Everyone loved him. He rode his little blue Datsun truck to every game Chrissy and I played. He never missed one. And every time Grandpa appeared, he was dressed in trousers, a dress shirt, and a tie. He was also never without his "Italian hat," a cap with a feather in it. Frank Coppola was always in the stands, talking to everyone and watching every minute of the game, joking with the parents of the other girls, jumping up for a hooray when one of us scored. No one was surprised when Frank Coppola was singled out for an award as "fan of the year."

At times he was like a second dad to me. Grandpa was always pulling me aside to say encouraging things. "You're going places, girl," he would say. "You're special." He loved to brag about me, or to say, "I told you so" after a winning basketball game. At my grandpa's funeral I wrote a letter to him, thanking him for teaching me so much about life and how precious it is.

Grandpa taught me the importance of family and tradition. He refused to watch movies, because he insisted that Hollywood was corrupt. But he loved Frank Sinatra, and would often brag about the time he met him and shook his hand. Whenever we listened to Sinatra together, Grandpa would say to me, "Now that's music, Care."

He was proud of being Italian—a pride he instilled in my mother, my sister, and me. He was proudest of all to be an American.

The cheerful look my grandfather wore in public faded into a grimace whenever he showed us his Purple Heart and Bronze Star. He told me that his parents had come across to Ellis Island from Italy when they were in their thirties, knowing almost no English. Their son ventured back across the Atlantic as a rifleman in Patton's 87th Infantry.

A veteran of the Battle of the Bulge, my grandfather would weep when his mind took him back into the battlefield, and he thought about all the friends he had left behind. He'd pull out his handkerchief, wipe his eyes, blow his nose, and say, "Carrie, I slept in trenches. It was so cold. I missed my family. I suffered and fought for your freedom. So don't *ever—ever—ever* let anyone take that freedom from you."

He said something else I never forgot.

"We had a lot of loudmouth atheists in our platoon," he said. "But on the frontline, when the bullets were zinging, the atheists would drop to their knees and pray." No matter how many times he told this story, Grandpa always cried when he got to this part. "They believed in God as much as I did when we were being shot at."

Grandpa was a handyman, who kept busy doing odd projects. He really taught me the value of hard work. Every morning he would go to McDonalds and grab his 50 cent coffee before coming to our house (which was a few houses away from his), always seeking another task that needed to be completed. He was so active—that's what kept him young. He got a call one morning at seven o'clock to fix the garbage disposal for a couple he had known for twenty-five years. He was happy to oblige. Frank Coppola had always said he wanted to die working—and that's just what he did. And when he died, I felt that I had lost a father.

After high school, I wanted my own place. As so many young people do, at least in theory, I wanted to be independent, to do my own thing, to live life as I wanted to live it. So I moved to Santa Barbara, where I attended Santa Barbara City College. My sister was nearby, studying on an Air Force ROTC scholarship at Westmont, a Christian liberal arts college. But when I wasn't visiting Chrissy, I felt very lonely.

Santa Barbara is a beautiful place, with sea fog, redwoods, and Spanish-style homes from the 1920s. I lived right on the beach and was within walking distance of my school. Somehow, though, all that beauty only added a touch of irony to what I felt inside. To all outward appearances, I was in paradise, but I was also the loneliest I have ever been in my life.

The reason for my loneliness was that I could not find a place to fit in. Even though I wasn't the best student, I was eager to learn, and I was naïve enough to think that college would be about being introduced to important ideas and books, and that my fellow students would be idealistic and high-minded, but I didn't find that to be true. The social scene created by my fellow students centered on weekend-binge-drinking, doing drugs, and sleeping around—which wasn't my scene at all. It struck me as a slow, lazy way to waste one's youth. Slacker has never been my style.

I took a break from school and returned to a northern San Diego suburb to be close to each of my divorced parents. If moving to Santa Barbara had been a mistake, moving back to San Diego proved to be a blessing. Here, I found community in a church (The Rock) that had hundreds of young people who felt as I did.

The relatively humble, chair-stacking ministry Miles had begun a few years before at San Diego State had exploded into a small city. The Rock was now a so-called "mega-church" with enormous spaces and 12,000 worshipers a week. I found more and more of my social life revolving around my friends and fellow worshipers at The Rock.

As the child of divorce, I sometimes felt that I had raised myself. But that really wasn't true, for I was parented and matured by my faith— the same faith that brought my parents back together into a new relationship focused on their daughters. And it was faith that helped me reorient my educational goals. A small local college, San Diego Christian College, offered me a basketball scholarship, and soon I was back to working on earning a college degree.

I got involved in two ministries at my church. One of them, "Luv-Em-Up," is a ministry for helping people with developmental and physical challenges. This ministry has had such a profound impact on me that it has opened up a possible career path to which I could happily devote my life. I love sports, and while I would love to be a sports reporter, I also love children, especially children with special needs. These two loves come together in the Special Olympics, an organization that is dear to my heart. This world really opened up to me when I got involved with Luv-Em-Up. This ministry assists disabled people of all ages in developing their own faith and knowledge of the Bible, while helping them bring their gifts to the world. There can be few better testaments to the faith we hold than witnessing the inherent human dignity of those among us who are the most challenged mentally and physically; there are few rewards that can mean so much as seeing the results and the joy in helping disabled people, and kids especially, achieve their goals.

The other ministry with which I got involved is "JC's Girls." This is a special ministry directed to women who are trying to transition out of the so-called "adult" entertainment industry, which is not only larger than you might think but also far more horrible. Some of JC's Girls have been strippers or involved in pornography. Others, like me, were there because we felt a calling to witness to these young women. The purpose of JC's Girls is not to judge or condemn, but to help these women heal through a personal relationship with Jesus Christ. We tell them that they are beautiful, and that Jesus loves them. Many of these girls have been through the ringer. When we reach them, or they come to us, their eyes are deadened by what they have seen and done, and their sense of self-worth and respect is down to absolute zero. Their souls feel crushed because they know they have taken a beautiful thing and, instead of using it as God intended, they allowed themselves to be exploited and degraded. Don't let anyone tell you that there are no victims in pornography. Anyone who tells you that has no idea what they're talking about. The very nature of pornography is abuse and exploitation and victimization; and for women, it is a modern form of slavery. Our goal is to set these women free and to help them find the inherent human dignity that is theirs. And believe me, I have seen them find it.

The Rock showed me where my true home was, and it was there that I found that all the values I had learned throughout my life had come together. My sister and teammates had taught me to fight and never give up. My grandfather had taught me that the independence some take for granted is hard won. My grandmother taught me about love and what a marriage should look like. My parents showed me that people could change. The Rock showed me where to find the truth, in faith and service.

Later, I would be asked by the Miss USA contest to identify my favorite song. I chose "I Was Here," by Lady Antebellum, which talks about making a difference, about doing something that matters, speaking out, and leaving your mark. Another song that was important to me was Nichole Nordeman's "Legacy," about leaving the world a testimony by which they can remember you.

I've always been a competitor, and I was psyched to set the world on its ear, to do something to put my stamp on life. That was my goal—and it was a goal I achieved in a way that I never could have imagined, or would have sought, and that sometimes made me think I was living through a new bloodless form of martyrdom, a sacrificial Christian thrown to the vicious and cruel media lions to be torn apart.

CHAPTER THREE

Just Another Sport

It all began, like so many other things in my life, with a dare. I was still seventeen when my friend Amanda said, "You're so pretty, Carrie. You really ought to compete in a beauty pageant."

I didn't want to offend her, but I didn't take to the idea at all. I was so into my sports. Then Amanda used the one word that she knew would hook me in. She called it a "competition." Some of my girl friends from church were competing at the local pageant level, so I started asking them questions. It's easy, they said. In many cases, they told me, all you have to do is enter an evening gown competition and answer a few questions; if you can model clothes with style and answer questions with finesse, you can set yourself up to win scholarships and attract job interviews. With the divorce and custody lawyers having taken so much of my parents' money, I especially needed scholarship money.

I imagined the pageant life would be a lot like sports. Eat right. Go to bed early (at least at the local level). Keep up your grades. Just as you are accountable to your team and coach, so I would also be accountable to my new team of handlers and directors. I would once again be working hard for something. Winning for me was everything—but this time, I'd be on my own, without my sister watching my back. I was ready, though, and the idea of competition was just too attractive. Before long I was asking, "How do I sign up?"

My first competition was Miss Teen Vista. When I told my parents and my sister about it, they looked at me like I was crazy. They knew me as the girl who scraped her knees sliding into second base, who got a fat lip jumping up for a rebound in the midst of flying elbows at a basketball game. But a beauty contest? Even I had to step back, after hearing their doubts, and confess I never thought I had what it took to win a beauty contest. I had watched them on television when I was little; I'd never imagined I'd be a participant in one. Still, even watching pageants as a little girl I'd been impressed with the poise of the participants. I always considered them role models—women little girls could look up to. I wanted to be a part of that if I could.

As competitions go, Miss Teen Vista did not ask a lot, which made the competitive athlete in me all the more infuriated when I lost, coming in as second-runner-up. If I was going to compete in pageants, I was going to compete to win. If I had to train harder—that's what I'd do. I asked the director what I had to do to win. She smiled at me in a way that made me even more desperate to win next time; in her mind, I should have been pleased to be runner-up. But second best has never been good enough for me, so I asked her, "What's the next step after winning Miss Teen Vista?" She told me the winners compete in Miss Greater San Diego Teen. That became my goal—not only to win Miss Teen Vista, but to win at the next level.

As luck would have it, the winner of Miss Teen Vista didn't want to go on to Miss Greater San Diego Teen. Neither did the first runner-up. So I stepped forward and said, "I'll do it, I'll compete."

When I told my parents I was doing another pageant, their disbelief had hardened into resistance. My mother asked, "Are you sure? You didn't win the first one. Are you really sure you want to try again, at a higher level?"

"Pageants really aren't your thing, Carrie," Dad would say. "You ought to pursue basketball. You're good at it."

But I was persistent. I told them I wanted to do this, and I meant what I said. I trained hard, preparing myself to be in top shape physically, mentally quick, graceful, balanced, and coordinated. Come the event, I felt I was ready for all the tests—the gown, the swimsuit, and the interview. And this time I won! The hard work, the determination, the perseverance had all paid off. I was on my way to the next level and already thinking of what I would have to do to win that one. I became Miss Greater San Diego Teen. When they gave me my sash and crown, with my whole family watching (Grandpa was crying, he was so happy for me), I was beaming with joy.

In winning that pageant, I brought to bear an old sports trick that I had been using for years. As a basketball player, I was able to pull off critical three-pointers by visualizing how the shot would go. I know a lot of athletes have this experience. If you can visualize what you need to do—sink that basket, make that punt, throw that strike—your mind and your body will get it done. When athletes talk about being "mentally tough" as well as "physically tough" that's partly what they mean. Part of it is not getting flustered, not losing your cool, not giving in when you're feeling tired or sore or afraid. But the other part is staying focused and visualizing what you need to do. It's a bit like acting. All successful athletes have to be actors to a certain degree, in the sense that they have to put their mind into the role of being a winner, of being successful, of acting out in their mind what they need to do on the field, or on the softball diamond, or on the basketball court. If you can do that, if you can play with confidence, you can be a winner. When I competed in the Miss Greater San Diego Teen pageant, I felt I was not only physically prepared, but I had my mental game on as well.

I was glad to win, of course, but I also recognized that some of the girls felt resentment against me. It wasn't just that they were upset to lose—I knew that feeling—it was that they regarded me as an outsider. I was more of a tomboy than a girly-girl—and tomboys weren't supposed to win pageants. Moreover, some of these girls were pageant veterans, who had competed from as early an age as six, and here I was, a newcomer walking away with the crown. But in my own mind, if I didn't have their experience, I had my own—the fierce competitiveness that came to me from sports and the inner strength that I felt I had developed from having to raise myself without the benefit of an intact home. I was dedicated. I worked hard. And as they say in sports, I was hungry—winning wasn't an option, it was a necessity; and I think I might have brought a bit more hard work to the pageant than some of the other contestants who thought they would cruise to victory.

Now I can imagine that some of you might roll your eyes at the idea of beauty pageants being about hard work. But let me tell you—they are. The dieting, the working out, all the physical aspects of the pageants are only a part of it. Even at the local level you have to survive a grueling interview with a panel of judges. You have to convince these judges that you have the poise and the knowledge to be a great Miss Whatever. For me, the next great "whatever" was Miss California Teen. As winner of Miss Greater San Diego Teen, I had free entry to the next level. If I was on my game now, I had to raise it to an even higher standard to compete successfully for the state title.

Part of that was schooling myself on the issues of the day. Traditionally in beauty pageants, judges avoided asking questions that were too political—perhaps for obvious reasons. But I had heard that some of the judges were veering in that direction—if for no other reason than to see if contestants could handle the pressure of coming up with a quick and articulate answer on subjects where feelings might run high and there were two sides to the story. So just to be on the safe side, I started watching FOX News with my Dad and reading the newspapers a little more closely.

I took etiquette classes. I started walking around the house with a book on my head. I even had a "walking instructor" who taught me a thousand things, but especially how to walk. Yes, you read that right. How to walk across the stage, hands in and open, shoulders relaxed, posture straight, chin up, eyes on the judges—make sure they remember you!

My instructor, Jim, a wonderful man who was openly gay, sized me up after first asking me to walk across the room: "Are you an athlete?"

"Yes." I was proud that Jim could tell it at a glance.

"Well," Jim said, "you need to get in touch with your feminine side."

He taught me how to walk like a beauty contestant, using first the technique of having me walk with a book on my head and then adding a kind of slinky style where each foot crosses in front of the other. He taught me when to smile, when not to smile, to put my hand on my hip at just the right moment, and to keep it down at my side while posing. I would work hard at that. And then I would go to basketball practice to work on my lay-ups and blocking. I lived in these two worlds. While sitting on the bench during a timeout in a game, I definitely was no beauty queen. At basketball practice, I was still Carrie the Jock. Then I would leave practice—and not tell my teammates where I was going for fear they would make fun of me—and go to see Jim, put that book back on my head, and try to walk like a beauty queen.

I also had help from Pam Wilson, a great coach and a woman of poise and intelligence, who had mentored me when I was competing as Miss San Diego Teen. She taught me which fork to use with which dish, and other points of etiquette. It was Pam, a veteran of the business, who taught me how to comport myself with confidence in an itsy-bitsy teeny-weeny bikini. She taught me how to stride elegantly in an evening gown, chin up, making eye contact with the judges and with the audience. She taught me to be myself—harder to do than you might think when you're on a stage or being grilled in an interview—and to use who I was to practical advantage. She taught me to appreciate my height and to stand tall with confidence. She instilled in me the importance of never forgetting who you are, and that what would make me a winner was not trying to become some generic beauty pageant contestant, but to be the best Carrie Prejean I could be. She encouraged me to be proud of my athleticism. When practicing questions at her house, she would remind me, "Carrie, remember who you are, where you came from, and your life experiences up until this point. You can answer any question! Do not be nervous, make them love you!" Those four special words—make them love you—were words I always remembered; they were a reminder that to win I had to bring out the best in myself.

I owe my instructors a lot, Jim and especially Pam. They brought about a transformation in me. They showed me how to go on stage and be a lady—the woman I was meant to be.

After winning Miss Greater San Diego Teen, I set my sights on the next level: Miss California Teen. Again, I went all out in my training and preparation. This time I came up just short: I was named first runner-up, which only whetted my appetite for more. From then on, what had been a lark became a passion for winning pageants. It was my new thing.

But there was a price for my new passion. Every time I didn't win, I felt bummed out. Failure in anything impelled me to work harder, try harder. But losing always hurt, and there were times when I wondered just how much more I could do. Still, from those low points, I resolved to push myself, always setting the bar just a little bit higher. I told myself I needed to improve in those areas where I displayed weakness. In my mind I would draw the line, and then push myself to live above it.

It was at this point that I enrolled in Santa Barbara City College, until the culture of endless parties—blenders and Margaritas, wine and beer, and the odor of marijuana in the hallways and in the parks—made me realize that I belonged in a place of order and competition. Pageants gave me that.

No sooner had I moved back home than Pam Wilson called. I was now old enough to compete for Miss Greater San Diego, the grown-up version of the Miss Greater San Diego Teen pageant. She encouraged me to go for it. Win that, she said, and who knows—you might become Miss California.

Pam had a warning for me as well. No girl in twenty-six years who had ever won the teen title, as I had done, had gone on to win the Miss Greater San Diego title. And so I thought, being the competitive girl I am, I've been off to college. I've grown up a little bit. I'll be the first.

If I thought I had worked hard before, it was nothing to the investment of training that I put into this competition. One of the great things about sports and competition is that hard work can pay off in tangible results; all the perspiration and determination, the dedication to staying focused on the prize, can lead to victory. Here the competition differed from the world of sports I was use to. I couldn't rely on teammates to throw me the rebound or pick me up when I got knocked down. I was on my own. Pam always told me, "Don't worry about the other girls. *You* are your competition." And the hard work paid off at last. I competed for the Miss Greater San Diego title—and I won.

Suddenly, the big time was dangling in front of me. Go on to win Miss California, and I might become Miss USA. But I soon found I was at a whole new level of competition, facing "girls" who were as old as twenty-six. I was still only nineteen years old and had been in the "beauty racket" for less than two years. Some of my competitors had been at it for a dozen years.

It was at this time that I heard there was a new director of Miss California, the owner of a modeling agency, who was innovative and shaking things up. His name was Keith Lewis. He was running Miss California with his firm, K2 Productions.

My first impression of Keith was very favorable. Keith is a handsome man who looks a little like the actor Kyle MacLachlan on *Desperate Housewives*, or maybe Matthew Perry. He is always nattily dressed, in that LA way that is both casual and businesslike. His hair is dark, thick, and always well styled. A tall, slender man, Keith has soft mannerisms belied by a professional demeanor that can be a little cold.

I soon learned that Keith was an openly gay activist who had been with his boyfriend for seven years. Despite the impression you might have of me from the more hysterical corners of the mainstream media, I took in all this information without judgment. The fact of the matter is, I liked Keith. I think he took to me as his protégé.

I saw a lot about him to respect. Keith is bright, has top connections in Hollywood, and is obviously a devoted father to his two children. That last point, being a good father, counts for a lot in my book, and I hoped his admirable devotion to his children might be reflected in a humane attitude to his contestants. In short, I sized up Keith as a very professional, very LA, entertainment entrepreneur who was going places—and might take me with him.

It wasn't long, however, before I began to see another side to Keith. At first I was told that he is known for being "tough." But another word might also be incompetent. In his few years as director, the pageant has been mired in controversies, lawsuits, and the discontinuation of his relationship with pageant winners. And it didn't start with me.

Christina Silva is a lovely girl of Ecuadorian descent from Los Angeles with short, dark hair and flashing eyes. I got to know her well as we competed against each other for the title of Miss California in LA's Orpheum Theater on the evening of November 25, 2008. Christina later told *Good Morning America* that on the night she won Miss California, "I saw my family by the balconies, and all I could do was cry and wave at them and say, 'Thank you God, thank you God.' It was an amazing, amazing feeling."

I watched all this as a second runner-up. Even though I lost, I, like everyone else that night, had tears of joy flowing for Christina. She was a great competitor, a surprise victor, and I knew how much this evening meant for her. The president of Ecuador actually called Christina's grandmother to congratulate the whole family on this great achievement for all Ecuadorian-Americans. That was the highlight of her reign. Unfortunately, it was her only highlight, because her reign was cut short—not through any fault of her own, but because of Keith.

Four days after she won the competition, Christina and her family were called to the Beverly Hills mansion of Keith's boyfriend, where Keith sat them down and said, "I don't know how to tell you this, but you are not the winner." The winner, Keith said, was another girl, Raquel Beezley. There had been, he said, an "accounting error."

"They never could explain their accounting error," Christina reported later on her blog, "but told me that if I didn't give up my crown, my personal integrity could be questioned, and my career could potentially suffer." She told *Good Morning America* that Keith had said, "We know you're faith-based and a woman of integrity, and we know you're going to do the right thing, right?"

Then they insisted that Christina herself call Raquel and break the news. "It was so bizarre," Christina said. "They kept saying, 'You have to tell her. You have to tell her. You are the honorable one.'" She was. Christina made the call to Raquel just thirty minutes after Keith told her she was fired.

The day after the competition, before any of this happened, Keith called me and asked me what I thought of the pageant. I told him honestly that I would never compete in a pageant again. I had worked so hard—as had all the finalists—that I didn't think I could psyche myself up to do it again, especially because I thought the panel's judgment was somewhat arbitrary. Christina is a lovely and accomplished girl, and while I was sincerely happy for her and thought she had done well, I didn't feel she should have won the competition.

. Four days later, I received another call from Keith.

"Carrie, we made a mistake," he said. "We crowned the wrong girl."

I was flabbergasted. "How does that happen?" I said. "The poor girl won, and you're going to take it away from her?"

"She didn't win," he said. "We can't let her keep it if she didn't win."

Now I felt butterflies in my stomach—they were mixed feelings of disgust at what Keith had done to Christina, giving her the crown only to snatch it away, and anticipation that he was about to tell me I was Miss California. I had to ask, "Did I win?"

"No, but this now means you are first runner-up."

At this, I had to laugh. I was seeing a pattern in my brief career as a beauty contestant. I had been first runner-up in Miss California Teen, and now Miss California. I wondered, briefly, if I ever went on to the Miss USA contest, would I be first runner-up there too? In pageantry there is a running joke about there being a first-runner-up curse. I seemed to be living it.

But what Keith told me next really set me back on my heels. He said he wanted me to come back to Los Angeles; they were going to reenact the Miss California finale, this time crowning the real winner. I was shocked—how fake, how phony, how utterly humiliating for everyone involved. He wanted me to hold hands with Raquel—it was all a big photo opportunity for the pageant to try to erase what they had done before in crowning Christina. But I didn't want to be a part of it. Even when Keith offered to buy me a train ticket up to Los Angeles, I politely declined the offer.

I also remember that from that day forward, I became a little suspicious of Keith Lewis. My respect for his professionalism was certainly beginning to fade. And I started to recognize that his reputation for toughness wasn't about strength and getting the most out of people; it was about being cold in making other people pay for his mistakes.

Sometimes people who get a reputation for being tough are really people who are harsh to others but forgiving of themselves. That's not very admirable. In my book, someone who is tough owns up to his mistakes as a person of character. I no longer saw that in Keith, especially as more details started to spill out about the pageant fiasco.

Keith's boyfriend's daughter later told me that she had been put in charge of the tabulations, and that it wasn't until between 2:00 and 3:00 a.m. the night before the pageant that Keith had given her the points the contestants had been awarded. The values he gave her were on a scale of one to five. He never made it clear, however, which end of the scale was for winners and which for losers. Was a "one" good and a "five" bad? Or was it the other way around? In any event, she mixed them up.

After the press interviewed a distraught Christina (who would later file a lawsuit), Keith's job as director, not to mention his personal investment in the California franchise of the Miss Universe organization, was on the line. There was talk that Paula Shugart, president of the Miss Universe pageant and ultimate boss of us all, would fire Keith.

In retrospect, it might have been better for everyone, Keith included, if she had. Instead, Paula told Keith that if he wanted to continue as director for another year he would have to find someone who would help the credibility of his pageant, someone who could make it run professionally.

The someone Keith found was Shanna Moakler.

Shanna was a first runner-up at Miss USA (as Miss New York), who went on to become Miss USA when the winner herself went on to win Miss Universe. Once linked romantically to Billy Idol, Shanna later had a daughter with Oscar de la Hoya. Splitting from the boxer, she filed a palimony suit against him demanding $62.5 million. Shanna is also known for posing nude as a *Playboy* model and for her now defunct reality TV show, *Meet the Barkers*, about her married life with Travis Barker, the heavily tattooed, Mohawk-haired drummer of Blink-182 (he later survived a plane crash that killed four others and left him recovering from severe burns); their apparently stormy marriage (now over) had been the stuff of tabloid headlines. Among the headlines was the story that Shanna and Paris Hilton had been involved in a physical altercation that led to police reports.

It seemed to me that Shanna Moakler might not have the right image to rehabilitate the pageant. At first, I worried that other state pageants might hold it against us that our state's co-directors were (a) someone who had managed to crown the wrong Miss California and (b) someone whose private life was all too public. Shanna's reputation was not what anyone would call "good," and she could in no way be seen as a role model for young women competing for Miss California. I'll confess, I was almost embarrassed to call her my director. I thought that pageants were about poise, grace, and character—that's what I had learned from Pam Wilson in the Miss Greater San Diego pageant, and that's why I found it worthwhile to compete. But I was just beginning to learn that in this world, celebrity counts for more than character. Having been the target of so many smears myself—and being far less than perfect—I don't like to revel in other people's misfortune or supposed scandals. I have also learned through painful experience just how much of what appears in print or on blogs can be completely false. But it did take me awhile to get used to the idea of Shanna helping to run the pageant. Later, when I finally decided to compete again, I knew I'd be working with Shanna, and I resolved to maintain a professional, respectful relationship with her.

I have to say, however, from the first moment I met her, Shanna did not come across as the calm, professional person you ask to bring order to a disorderly house. Shanna was a little rough around the edges and didn't seem to have the sort of punctuality and tact required of a person in a position of authority. For instance, Shanna was more than an hour late for a meeting at orientation at the Miss California pageant. Some of the girls were laughing together, saying Shanna had been too hung over from drinking and partying the night before to turn up on time. Whether or not that was true, it's not my idea of professionalism.

I thought I was done with pageants, after the Christina Silva fiasco, but Keith was persistent. He had two objectives: he wanted me to sign on with a modeling agency in Los Angeles (this was the agency that later set me up with a photographer who released photos of me to the media, which were meant to undercut my credibility as a Christian woman), and he wanted me to reenter the Miss California Pageant. I had told him firmly that I wasn't doing pageants anymore, but he kept calling—at least once a month. Each time it was the same: "Please come back." He knew, he told me, I would make a great Miss California. He went on to say that I had the makings of a great Miss USA. Two months before the Miss California pageant, he called one last time, telling me that I needed to reconsider. He said he would waive the entry fee—$1,500—if I agreed.

I thought about it, talking to Keith, walking around my Dad's house with a cordless phone. My modeling career was taking off, I was very busy, and I had been adamant that pageants were behind me. But Keith finally won me over. After all, I thought, why not give it one last shot? Just like the professional athlete who gets lured out of retirement with the hope that this time he might win it all, I thought it was worth a try. This would be my final competition—that was settled—and that meant I needed to leave nothing behind. I would go all out, and this time I would win—I was already visualizing victory—and when that happened I would strive to be the best Miss California they ever had!

Something else came to my attention soon thereafter, though I paid it little mind. Keith was the executive producer of an award-winning documentary that premiered at the 2007 Sundance film festival, *For the Bible Tells Me So*, which profiles prominent parents of gays and argues that religious groups opposed to homosexuality have got it all wrong. Keith gave the contestants copies and told them to watch it and tell him what they thought of it. The documentary got a lot of play because it came out around the time of the campaign for Proposition 8, a state ballot measure that defined marriage the traditional way, as an exclusive relationship between one man and one woman. California had become ground zero for this debate, because in San Francisco, Mayor Gavin Newsom had created a political firestorm by allowing city hall to marry gay people in defiance of California law. Already in 2000, California voters had overwhelmingly passed Proposition 22, clarifying the state's constitutional definition of marriage to be exclusively between a man and a woman. But in mid-2008, the California Supreme Court claimed to have discovered a "right" to gay marriage in the state constitution, which obviously no one had ever seen there before. Many Californians began to worry that a likely result of this "right" would be the loss of tax-exemptions for churches if they refused to marry same-sex couples, and the mandating of same-sex values in public schools. The words of Newsom haunted the political landscape: Gay marriage is coming, he said, "whether you like it or not."

Californians didn't like it. They especially didn't like having an issue that had such deeply religious and social dimensions being decided for them by judges.

Finally, in November 2008, after a long and testy campaign fought out in public protests, debates, and controversial radio and television ads, California voters went to the polls to vote on a constitutional amendment defining marriage as between a man and a woman. My view was the same as the majority of Californians who voted on the issue. My pastor, Miles McPherson, vocally supported Proposition 8—and did so calmly, with a sense of compassion, and without a trace of ill will. I liked to think that I held my own beliefs the same way. I believed that the traditional definition of marriage should not be changed. By the same token, I am not bothered by the idea of gay people choosing to live their lives together as they see fit—just as Keith and his boyfriend did—just don't call it marriage.

I was not then, nor am I now, aspiring to be the next Anita Bryant. I am comfortable with all God's children. Civil unions between gay people, at least as a matter of law, have always been fine with me. If asked, I would have told you that I believed that gay couples should have visiting rights in the hospital, just like everybody else. But like most Californians and a certain candidate for president from Illinois, I believed then and I believe now that marriage should be a legally recognized sacrament between a man and a woman. If that makes me a bigot, so is Barack Obama.

But in the fall of 2008, Proposition 8, though it was something that all Californians had to have opinions on, was far from the forefront of my mind. My attention was tightly focused on winning Miss California. I wasn't researching the political and religious history of marriage, the rulings of the California Supreme Court, or the historical and judicial debates over California's constitution. I was concentrating on how to win the swimsuit and evening gown competitions, and how to nail the final question of the Miss California Pageant.

The big day came, and once again, I kept making the early eliminations. I made the top fifteen, then the top ten, and finally the top five. Would I be a runner-up yet again? I was ready to win and had concentrated on sharpening my focus through every round of the competition. I also did my best to help my roommate. On the day of our interviews, she was really sick and couldn't even get out of bed. I almost didn't make it to my own interview, because I spent an hour coaxing her out of bed and then helping her get dressed and apply her make-up. We both just barely made it to our interviews. Unfortunately, she later ended being hospitalized for her illness, though I'm glad to say she recovered, with her mom providing her with tremendous support.

The last competition was, of course, the on-stage question segment. I was asked about leadership—a pretty dull topic, but at least I wasn't asked about world peace.

I answered that while I was at San Diego Christian College I had had the chance to mentor other girls. I specifically mentioned how we kept each other accountable with the Lord. It was a direct and honest answer, and in retrospect, perhaps a risky one. But as I gave it, I saw not a flicker of resistance from the judges.

As it turned out, it was a winning answer, at least with judges at the state level. In fact, the judges said they loved my answer; they loved me talking about the importance of faith. They told me they had me pegged from the beginning as the likely winner, that they thought I stood out from the competition—which was flattering. And they said, "When you spoke about the Lord in that last question, we loved you!"

I had never prepared so hard for a pageant in my life, and I knew how much of the credit belonged to Pam Wilson, my pageant coach and mentor. I wept with pride and joy for her, for me, and for God's blessings, when they bestowed the sash on me, handed me the bouquet, and crowned me Miss California.

I was ecstatic. Words cannot describe my joy at winning the crown. I lived the dream of some girls that night: I slept with my crown and sash next to my bed. In the morning, I drove home to San Diego, just in time to attend chapel at my college, where I was invited to speak. I told my fellow students that I gave all the glory and honor to God, and that I hoped I could do my part to uphold his glory in this new public role I had been given. I told them I felt sure that God had chosen me to represent not only the state of California, but him.

I knew that role might grow. As Miss California, I was our state's representative to the Miss USA pageant, and already at the celebration dinner after the crowning, everyone was talking to me about winning Miss USA.

I couldn't wait to go to Las Vegas and compete.

CHAPTER FOUR

Planet Hollywood

I suddenly had a team, a family. Or so I thought. I had Keith and Shanna; I had Pam, who helped me all along the way; and Debbie Dodge, who guided me through fashion and wardrobe (Pam and Debbie were my chief counselors); I had an accent modification coach (Keith said I sounded like I was from the Midwest, and I needed to talk like Miss California—whatever that meant); and I still had Jim, my walking instructor. Keith was ecstatic I had won. He treated me as his pet project, the girl he was molding and shaping to win the heart of the country—and perhaps, as Miss Universe, the world.

But my helpers could only do so much. It was up to me to close the deal for the next level of competition, to win Miss USA. And so I worked on the mind game, the mental and emotional preparation that

I think is the key to winning at anything. I worked hard, I visualized victory, and I told myself that nothing could keep me from going all the way and becoming Miss USA.

While I was preparing, a lot of friends, well-wishers, and people knowledgeable about the pageant told me I was the frontrunner, the "girl to beat." Some might have considered this bad luck. Not me. It fed my desire to win. I convinced myself that if I acted like I was already Miss USA, my inner confidence would be seen by others, and it would carry me through.

But there is a lot more happening in a contest like this than just emotional preparation. I worked out as if I were training for the state basketball finals instead of a beauty pageant. I kept studying the newspapers and watching FOX News with intense interest. I somehow expected, as I told my dad, that I might get a question with a little political twist. He thought I might be asked: "Do you think America is ready for its first female president?" We thought of every conceivable question—except the one put to me by Perez Hilton.

I could feel the stakes getting higher. The fact that the competition would be in Las Vegas seemed appropriate. I had invested months of my life and my pride in what was turning out to be one big gamble.

The media scrutiny was far more than anything I had experienced in previous pageants. Girls from big states, like Texas, Florida, and my own California, got tons of attention—no doubt because of the big media markets in those states. I tried my best to answer questions from the press with calm confidence. I tried not to act cocky, but inside I convinced myself that all this attention was preparing me to win. It probably helped my chances that most of the judges were from Hollywood. I thought it might give me an advantage that they were acquainted with Shanna, since she was associated with the Hollywood scene. I even remember Keith Lewis telling me, "Carrie, you're the favorite—you're going to win this thing!"

As Keith showered me with confidence-building compliments, Shanna inadvertently undermined my confidence. It started out as sort of a good cop, bad cop routine—though pretty soon they double-teamed me as bad cops. Shanna blasted off many emails telling me that this or that about me was just not right. She wanted my hair platinum blonde. And she told me I needed work done on my face. "You need restalyne for those smile lines," she said, as if a 21-year-old could really have facial lines that required attention.

It would have been one thing if Shanna had been polite, with the manners I always expected were part of being a beauty queen, and made suggestions like, "What if we try you hair this way?" But Shanna's style was blunt, and it came across as mean. She once said, "No one liked your hair at Miss California. It was over 300 colors. We need to change it. I want you *BLONDE*—like Gwyneth Paltrow!" And she followed this up with pictures of Gwyneth Paltrow, criticizing my hair in comparison. Apparently, being a platinum blond was a prerequisite for winning. Shanna would tell me, "You do *not* have Miss USA in the bag!" At other times she would get exasperated, saying, "I'm washing my hands of you. I'm going to focus on the 2010 Miss California Pageant."

Criticizing my hair was one thing, but here I was, an athlete, working out like crazy, and Shanna, and eventually Keith, kept back-biting me about how I needed to work out even more and diet better. It's one thing for a coach to push a player and demand more in a productive way. But it's quite another to belittle someone just for the sake of criticizing—and that's what I felt Shanna and Keith were doing. They were not offering useful advice that would actually advance me to my goal, they were indulging in personal, verbal abuse. Maybe that's what they meant by "tough," but they came across as people trying to justify their roles as my "handlers." Then Shanna would remind me that I needed to be "grateful." She would take me out shopping on Rodeo Drive, telling me that other title holders didn't have great directors like her and Keith, and that I should appreciate them taking me shopping at places like Chanel. Frankly, I didn't see why I should be grateful for those things, when I got so little real support from my directors; I knew good coaches, and I wouldn't have put Shanna and Keith in that category. I also felt they were pushing me in directions I didn't want to go— botox, bleach, and boob jobs. I ended up giving in on some points, but I wanted to win as me, as the person God made me, not as the person Shanna and Keith wanted me to be.

I had a nutritionist in whom I would confide, and he was extremely sympathetic. He, unlike Shanna and Keith, knew what I was doing and always gave me great advice. One thing he said, which made a lot of sense to me, was that if I was to keep my competitive edge, I had to stay focused, filter out the negative, and concentrate on the positive. I know it might sound like a cliché, but it's also easier said than done, and Shanna and Keith weren't making it easy for me to achieve that necessary focus.

I tried to tell myself that Shanna meant well, that her style was shock and awe, a boot camp for beauty queens. But I frankly doubted some of her judgments; it was hard to tell which of her suggestions were really in my best interest and which were merely her aggressive nature and ego on overdrive. If I had let her get to me, I would have been utterly demoralized.

A magazine which dealt with pageantry, modeling, and fashion did a wonderful article on me, called "Beyond Beauty." They featured my involvement with the Special Olympics. Before we got all the arrange-ments nailed down, though, Shanna kept putting them off, telling me that I shouldn't be focused on magazine articles at this point. I needed to pay attention to my appearance—focusing on my hair, my tan, and my diet. Our priorities were just completely different.

I held my ground on some issues—no Botox for me, thanks just the same. On other issues, though, I just had to give in. To please Shanna, I let them take me to a salon in Beverly Hills and dye my hair platinum blonde. I thanked them, but I just didn't feel right. I thought, *Why am I trying to change my look when I've gotten so far just by being who I am?*

Foolish me. I had no idea what they would change next.

The Miss California Pageant allowed me to pick out a gown of my choice, which was paid for by a generous sponsor, and willingly took care of my hair (even when I didn't want them to), and helped me with make-up when I was in Los Angeles. They also had a wonderful, gen-erous jewelry sponsor who decked me out in beautiful diamonds. All that was very nice, and I was very grateful, but you'd be surprised about how much was actually left to me to do on my own. The pageant had no wardrobe sponsor—I had to find one myself and ask if I could wear their clothes to the Miss USA Pageant. They had no travel man-ager. I had to do that myself. The idea that I would have everything right at my fingertips was utterly wrong. For being in charge of such a big event, it often seemed that the Miss California Pageant officials were disorganized and operating on the cheap and on the fly. Two for-mer Miss Californias encouraged me, saying that being Miss California was all about what you chose to make of it; that it was really up to you to do whatever you wanted. That was fine and good, but it might also have been a polite way of saying, "Don't expect much support or direction—it's up to you."

One former Miss California, Meagan Tandy, was not only a huge help when I needed advice, she was also bluntly honest in her assessment of Keith. She told me flat out, repeatedly, that Keith was an "evil" man. She said when she was Miss California that Keith was always unavailable when she needed him and verbally abusive to her whenever they did connect. For example, he told her angrily that she was representing *his* brand and could do no appearances if her skin wasn't perfectly acne-free. Things got so bad that Meagan had her father intervene to protect her. Keith was no longer allowed to call Meagan directly; if he wanted to talk to her, he had to go through her dad. I found her stories pretty scary, but given my own recent experiences, absolutely believable.

When Keith did not provide me with a wardrobe sponsor, I found my own in Los Angeles. The store's owner graciously offered to let me try on whatever I wanted to wear, run it by the pageant directors, model it for the camera, and return it when I was done. Keith agreed it was a good idea. He joined me at the store. Then to my shock, he actually joined me in the dressing room. I tried to shoo him away, but Keith wouldn't leave. He stood there, watching me change, even when I stripped down to my underwear, standing before the changing mirror.

Earlier, in the Miss California pageant during which Keith presided over the crowning of the wrong girl, he had let a camerawoman roam around where girls were undressing, as if we were NFL players in a locker room after a game. He had no sense of boundaries.

There were some other unsettling moments.

A few days after I won Miss California, I was called into a meeting with Keith and Shanna, Roger Neal (the Pageant spokesman), as well as with a trainer and a nutritionist. They asked me to get into my bathing suit, another teeny-weeny bikini. I changed and came out into Shanna's living room, feeling goose bumps rise on every bare spot of my body. Keith walked around me, looking me up and down appraisingly. He stopped and stared at my butt. For a long time. He touched me on the butt, then ran his hands around my hips, looked at my butt again, touched it again, ran his hands around my hips again, and examined each of my breasts.

I felt heat rising from my face. I didn't believe that Keith, as a gay man, was doing any of this because he was turned on by it. But I do believe he was telling me something. I got the sense that he was saying that because he was the co-director, he could do whatever he wanted with me. He was saying: *You're mine now, and I'm going to fix you, and shape you and mold you however I want.*

And then he said, "Have you ever thought of getting a boob job?"

"Yeah," I said, "every girl has thought of it, but I'm not sure I want one."

He told me that he had paid for some of the past Miss Californias to have boob jobs, and that I should seriously consider having the surgery. "I really think you need it," he said. "I'll look up some doctors for you, and we'll get it going." He told me the pageant would pay for it and made it clear it had to happen soon. He also said he knew a doctor in Los Angeles who could give us a discount.

So I complied with Keith's request and met with the doctors, and then had the procedure done. Going into surgery was scary, but, thankfully, the recovery was not at all painful—at least physically. It was, however, later used by Keith and others to try to embarrass me.

After I became politically radioactive, Keith volunteered for the CBS *Early Show* that breast implants are "not something that we endorse, nor is it something that we suggest. But when we meet with the title-holder when she's crowned Miss California, we put to her a litany of questions about how she feels about herself, what she feels she needs to work on, what she may need to change, what is good, what is not good."

Actually, the only thing Keith Lewis put to me were his two big hands and an insistent request, bordering on a demand, that I get breast implants. But Keith figured that in making this false revelation he would hurt my credibility with the public—that he would make me look false and unchristian. It is amazing how little it takes to create a scandal in this country, but Keith's gamble paid off, in part because after my honest answer to Perez Hilton, I became a political hate figure, and certain talking heads were only too eager to join in the chorus of abuse.

For instance, Keith Olbermann went on a rant on his national television show, ridiculing me for being a "woman who is partially made out of plastic." Olbermann and others suggested I was somehow a hypocrite, a bad Christian, for changing my body. I don't regret having had the surgery, even if I did it reluctantly. It was a choice I had to make, and I made it; and as with all my choices, I'm prepared to stick by it. But I do regret allowing myself to be so easily pushed and led around by Keith.

Unfortunately, there would be much more of that to come.

Now that I was Miss California, I expected to be the state's ambassador at events from the Mexican border to Oregon. I expected to have my hands full with travel, bookings, hotels, plane trips, all to support the causes that benefit people in need of healing or opportunity. My expectations soon began to meet reality. When it came to appearances, I was pretty much on my own. I would receive an email from Lilly in Keith's office with a list of events going on in Hollywood, along with a note asking me to pick the one that I wanted to attend. I remember seeing on the list a George Lopez event to raise money to combat kidney disease. I always liked George Lopez, so I decided to go.

To my surprise, I had to do all the work of scheduling that event by myself (my Mom helped); and I was completely on my own—no one from Keith's office went with me; no press agent, no chaperone, no Keith. Event appearances were obviously not a big deal to Keith and his team, and we certainly thought about them differently. I thought being Miss California was about serving, doing community work, and representing the state. When I won, I made a list of things I wanted to do as Miss California. I wanted to visit the troops, work with children in need, go to hospitals, meet the governor—all things I thought a Miss California would normally do. But it soon became apparent to me that this wasn't Keith's view of Miss California at all; his view was that Miss California was Miss Hollywood, and it was Hollywood events and Hollywood causes that he wanted me to attend and support, insofar as he cared about events at all. Prior to the Miss USA Pageant, Shanna and Keith would tell me, "It's not about making appearances, it's about winning Miss USA."

When I got back and looked at the list again, I realized that what Lilly had sent me—including all fifty-three possible events—was simply the Hollywood News Calendar. It contained events like Britney Spears's birthday party, to which I had not actually been invited, where I would have been of no use, and which was not exactly a place where I thought the state of California needed to fly its flag (or me, my sash). Oddly, the few events that seemed appropriate to me and that I was interested in were often, I was told by Keith's office, at capacity (like the Grammy Awards, to which Shanna said she couldn't get me tickets), or were not worth my time, or were otherwise bad ideas.

Events that had nothing to do with Hollywood simply didn't interest them. For example, loving sports as I do, I wanted to go to a book-signing event for the Olympic swimmer Michael Phelps. I thought there was a perfectly clear rationale for it, too: he had represented our flag and country at the Olympics, and I was representing our state as Miss California. The response? Keith's office replied: "It's simply a book signing. He'll [Phelps] be there for one or two hours just signing books. People have to wait in line for a wristband, there's no pre-confirming or anything like that. The guy said a lot of people are camping out in line. There's no red carpet. It's pointless really." Later, after Michael and I became good friends (though not the torrid romantic partners the gossip sheets tried to make us out to be), we had a big laugh about this. Less funny, though, was my fear that I wasn't fully doing my job as Miss California because of the reluctance of Keith and his team to book me into appropriate charitable or community events.

This went from a minor worry to a major headache. In Las Vegas, I would later see that Miss Texas, Miss Florida, and other girls from big states had teams that ensured they were smartly scheduled in appropriate appearances; their pageant directors made sure they attended events where they could do some good. In my case, I had a longstanding relationship volunteering for the Special Olympics. This was independent of my pageant life, but there was no reason why it should remain outside of it; as Miss California I thought I could do so much more to bring attention to this incredible cause. The Special Olympics touched me in a special way because it brought together my love of athletics, my Christian values, and my respect for the developmentally disabled. I thought that visiting children's hospitals and attending events for the Special Olympics were exactly the kinds of things a Miss California should do. But Keith's office took little interest, or even notice, of something that I thought could be a good work *and* a public relations bonanza for the Miss California organization.

In December 2008, an event caught my eye: a fundraiser for a prominent children's hospital was listed in the Hollywood News Calendar. So I phoned the hospital on my own initiative and asked if I could help them with their fundraising. They said they would love to have me.

When I told Keith Lewis about the fundraiser, he never responded. As it was with the crowning of the wrong girl as Miss California in the Christina Silva debacle, I began to see that Keith was very unorganized. Here he was, in Los Angeles right next to all these events, but he couldn't schedule an appearance or even bother to show up for one. Keith and the pageant officials had told me from the beginning of my reign as Miss California that I would be free to do the events I wanted to do. All they required was that I email them and let them know. I never had to get anything approved, I just needed to use my own good judgment and bring a chaperone with me. That supposed freedom was the tradeoff for the pageant doing so little to support and assist me.

Keith did manage to get me to one event on the same day I was to go to the children's hospital. It was a red carpet event for a glammy, high-concept clothing store called Imperial Planet.

Here is the email I received from Keith's office:

Plan on meeting at Keith's tomorrow at 11 a.m. Keith is going to take you to look at some gowns before shopping at Imperial Planet. You can dress casual for shopping, but you may want to wear something that is easy to take off. Maybe bring a pair of high heels and strapless bra.

There is going to be a lot of press at Imperial Planet so you should dress appropriate for Red Carpet (Cocktail attire). If you are unsure of what to wear, it may be a good idea to bring a couple different options, and Keith can help you select an outfit.

DON'T FORGET YOUR SASH!!!

Keith and his people seemed to think about every detail having to do with clothes, hair, and appearances. Only a few things were left out, like the "what" and the "why." (Soon, I would find out, the "where" could be missing, too.)

So I went. I walked around Imperial Planet, dodging waiters carrying appetizers and people dancing to the live DJ, all this between stacks of denims and button-downs. Keith didn't go to the event because he had dinner plans with his boyfriend. But there seemed to be no reason for me to be there either. Some girls might think being a beauty pageant winner is about going to trendy Hollywood openings, but that wasn't what I had in mind at all. I didn't want to party, I wanted to do things—I wanted to make a difference in people's lives— as Miss California. I had a horrible sinking feeling, as I stood there watching the cool, the hip, the beautiful people munching appetizers and dancing, that I had made a mistake. If this was what being Miss California was going to mean, I should never have bothered to compete. I had never been looking for a ticket to Hollywood events; I had been looking for a way to serve causes that meant something to me and that could help others.

When my Imperial Planet ordeal was over, I left for the children's hospital event with an address Keith's office had finally provided me. Wearing my sash and placing my crown on the passenger seat, I drove my Jetta to the hospital. At one point, I had to fill up my tank at a convenience store in the middle of Los Angeles—and only when I started to pump the gas did I remember to remove my sash. I wonder what people made out of that!

I finally got there only to learn that Keith's office had given me the wrong address. The actual fundraiser was far off-site, a good two hours away, too far to make it in time. At that moment, I gave into a little self-pity: *Why didn't Keith and his team give me more support? Why was I alone? Why did I have to do all this by myself?* It was getting dark, the neighborhood around the hospital was not the best, and, as usual, I had no chaperone that night.

The night managers at the hospital were kind. Knowing I couldn't make it to the fundraising event, I asked them if there was anything I could do at the hospital—and they told me there surely was. My crown and sash would make a big impression on some little patients.

Because I had been sent to the wrong address, I had the priceless opportunity to spend two hours visiting the beautiful children of the cancer ward. Some of the little girls were bald. All of them were cute. And they oohed and aahed as if a real Disney princess had showed up in their room when they saw me wearing my crown and sash. The teenage boys lit up when I walked into the ward, grinning at their good luck. They couldn't wait to click a picture with me on their cell phones to send to all their friends. I visited some of the more severe cases— children who had suffered relapses or were facing their last chance to beat the disease. Their lives were on the line. But I was touched, moved, overjoyed to have been there for them that night. For me the contrast between Planet Hollywood and the cancer ward of the children's hospital could not have been starker. I knew where I was needed and where I wasn't.

There was no doubting that I was straddling two worlds. Here I was in a short cocktail dress (I threw a jacket over my shoulders to cover up a bit), in high heels, and made up like a Barbie doll. I would rather have gone as Miss California the helper, in a business suit (crown, sash, and all), rather than as Miss California the hot new thing.

To my mind the real worth of a pageant is not about celebrity, because celebrity is an illusion created by the media puffing up people who are no more special than you or I. But celebrity can be used in ways that help people. There was no mistaking that the crown on my head acted like magic, bringing a glow of happiness to a ward full of sick kids who might not have had very much to be happy about. I firmly believe that God had a plan for me that night, and I had plenty of time to reflect on it after I left the hospital, while the children were saying sweet good nights to their parents. I thanked the hospital staff who had done so much to make this visit such a wonderful one, and then sometime after midnight checked myself into a hotel. There I came to some grim conclusions.

Keith was supposed to be a professional; he was supposed to know something about pageants. He was in charge of running the Miss California organization, and yet he seemed to take no interest in events where I could use my title to do some good; his office came across as disorganized and dysfunctional, existing only so he could exploit girls like me for whatever celebrity he gained from it. That might have represented his interests, but I didn't think it served my best interests or the interests of the pageant. It certainly didn't represent the ideal of service that I thought being Miss California was all about. The one good thing his office had done for me that night was a mistake—a mistake that had embarrassingly sent me to the wrong event, but that had, ironically, opened a path far better than anything I could have imagined.

Keith might have valued my going to Imperial Planet, but that was not my scene, and what possible use was it for me to go there? When I visited the kids, I felt that was where I should be. I felt like the Lord was saying, "This is what you're supposed to be doing." It's about serving, not glamour. Certainly not Imperial Planet. Later, in the spring, I had become so bothered by the lack of planning or structure in my schedule that I sent a memo to Keith's office:

> Just a thought. I was wondering if the . . . website could have a "book Miss California USA for an appearance" section. I think that would be great for organizations to go on the website and know the information on how to request me for an event . . . . Just a thing to think about, don't know if you were already thinking about doing something like this. It was just fresh in my mind, and I thought I'd ask.

To make it crystal clear, I even posted an example from the website of the Miss America Organization. I got no response.

While I was preparing to compete for Miss USA, Shanna invited me to spend the night at her house (Travis Barker's house) in a celebrity neighborhood, where, she told me, Britney Spears lived right down the hill from her—very exciting—*not.* I'm not saying I can't be as star-struck as the next girl, but the whole Hollywood-celebrity-tabloid culture was pretty far removed from me. If Shanna was *US Weekly*, I was *Sports Illustrated*; we lived in different worlds.

I spent the whole day with Shanna. We went to dinner, and I really got to know her. She was much friendlier in this setting than she had been before, but she used such coarse language, and she was so full of gossip about Hollywood, that I felt a bit alienated from her, too. I was twenty-one; she was in her mid-thirties. I was supposed to look to her for leadership, but I found that a hard proposition to swallow.

While I was getting ready for bed, Shanna, who is a night owl and likes to sit up late blogging, asked if I wanted to watch a movie in her enormous movie theater room. I said sure. But she had another thing she wanted to talk about—my answer at the Miss California Pageant where I had spoken about leadership in the context of mentoring girls at my college. She said I answered these questions well, but there was a little too much about God.

She turned blunt: "Don't talk about God anymore. It just makes people feel really uncomfortable."

Then she got blunter: "Really, I don't want you talking about God, because not everybody believes in God, so don't talk about him anymore."

I didn't want to get into a big discussion about this with her. I told her I was a Christian, God is a big part of my life, and that when it came to answering the question about leadership, I had replied as honestly as I could.

But as far as providing a witness, I have to confess I was pretty muted. When she asked if I would stop talking about God, I didn't reply. I just changed the subject.

My response (or non-response) bothered me then, and it bothered me for a long time afterward. I felt as if I had failed myself, as if I had been given a chance to stick up for my faith and completely blown it. The first Christians sacrificed their lives rather than burn incense on the altar of Caesar. And here I was saying basically, "Okay, sure."

The "God question" had arisen just a few weeks after my surgery, when I was filling out my Miss USA application. It included questions like: "Where do you go to school?" and "What do you like to do?"

One question stood above all others: "If you could have lunch with any person, dead or alive, who would it be?"

I answered God.

Now I know some people might find this a bit silly. After all, where would you go to eat with God? Taco Bell?

But there was a deeper meaning for me. Who do I admire most? Who can tell me what I need most to know about my life and what to do?

So I gave an explanation of how I would like to thank God face to face for all that he has done for me. I wrote about how amazing it would be just to be with him.

I explained all this to Keith's assistant in an email: "If I got to see God face to face, I would thank Him personally for His sacrifice, grace, and love for me. Just being in His presence alone, I might be speechless."

No sooner had I sent in my application for Keith's approval than I got a call. Why? "Because," Keith said, "God is not really a person."

"Well," I said, "I'll put Jesus. Will that make it less confusing?"

Keith answered, "A lot of people don't believe in Jesus."

"I'm a Christian," I told him, "I believe in Jesus."

"I'm not comfortable with you putting Jesus," he said. "Why don't you pick an answer that's appealing to most people? Why don't you pick George Bush?"

George Bush! From commander of the universe to commander in chief was a long step down. No offense to the president. After all, when Bush was asked his favorite philosopher, he replied, "Christ, because he changed my heart." He didn't say Richard Nixon.

"Okay," Keith said, trying another tact, "change it to 'God, whichever god you wish it to be.'"

Once again, I went along. I took God out of my application entirely—better that than making it "whichever god you wish it to be"—and instead wrote that I would like to have lunch with California's first lady, Maria Shriver.

Changing my answer added to my disappointment in myself. I talked to a good friend about it and said I felt like God had brought me up to this point, but when it came to the test, I dropped Him, because Keith Lewis told me to. A good friend, Juliana, told me, "Carrie, don't beat yourself up over it. As a Christian girl, you will have an opportunity to make up for it." I hoped so. I resolved that I wouldn't compromise my beliefs again.

One way I could keep my reslove was through the events I set up for myself. One was a visit to a retirement home for former pro-football players and their spouses. My paternal grandparents Anita and Billy came with me. I talked about them, about how much I had learned from them, how they had instilled in me the need to stay true to who I am and to my faith, how they had taught me how to enjoy life, and how they had helped me appreciate the meaning of family. They have been married for fifty-seven years, and have twenty-one grandchildren and twenty-one great-grandchildren.

Sure it was personal, and I was glad to be able to honor my grandparents in that way, but it was also a message appreciated by the audience. Retirement homes weren't on Keith's Hollywood List, but I definitely had the impression that Miss California was more appreciated there, or at hospitals, than she might be at Imperial Planet. I told Keith's office assistant about the event. She replied in an email, "Awww how nice. I'll def include in the newsletter."

But if that event was down-home, I was soon to be thrust onto a national stage: the Miss USA Pageant in Las Vegas. This was the climax of it all—and it would result in my making headlines that shocked me as much as they shocked anyone else.

CHAPTER FIVE

Not Exactly "World Peace"

The two-and-a-half weeks in Las Vegas for the Miss USA Pageant were a crazy blur of appearances, press conferences, and charity events. At each event, I sized up the competition, fifty other beautiful women (all fifty states are represented, plus the District of Columbia). Only one of us would leave as the winner. I was determined to stay focused and not let any drama with the other girls get me off my game.

As unreal as everything was—Las Vegas with its fake Eiffel Tower and replica New York skyline—living for a long time in the spaceship environment of the Planet Hollywood Hotel only made it weirder. I suddenly found myself in the middle of a mob scene, paparazzi, and an assortment of followers everywhere we went. For once, I had a chaperone, as well as security. I also had a roommate, Aureana, who was Miss Hawaii.

We all soon fell into a routine together. The Miss USA Organization was already using us as beauty queens, sending us to wholesome events. Between the appearances and outings to see Cirque du Soleil and other shows, I was working my butt off. We couldn't go down to the gym or the pool, but we could exercise in our rooms and in the hallways. We were up at 6:00 a.m., to breakfast by 7:00 a.m., then five hours of rehearsing every aspect of the pageant. Lights out at midnight. It was tough and weird, like enlisting in the Navy SEALs, only with paparazzi and neon lights.

The pressure began to wear on some of the girls. Some of them were actually starving themselves. Some had brittle, fake smiles and looked as if they were on the verge of having a breakdown. The whole time I kept telling myself that I was tough enough to make it through: "I'm an athletic girl; I'm not a pageant girl. I can take this."

The fake environment was amplified by the fake beauty—fake hair, fake eyelashes, fake tans—everything about the pageant and our host city of Las Vegas was artificial and fake. But I couldn't be too judgmental, because I was one of them, with my new boobs and my platinum-blonde hair. I thought if my new little friends would help me win, then so be it. I'll put on my best smile and be fake, too. But as determined as I was to win, and even as I had gone along with the hair and with the surgery, I was equally determined that I wouldn't let the pageant change who I really was. When this was over, I'd still be Carrie Prejean of Vista, California—maybe Carrie Prejean, Miss USA, representing my country to the world, but Carrie Prejean the real person all the same.

Cliques began to form. I had mine. I hung out with the West Coast girls—they had a more laid-back attitude, and they were fun. The East

Coast girls formed their own little group as well. In the most casual way, everyone was always looking to check out what the other girls were wearing—and then one-up them.

The one thing everyone asks me is whether the atmosphere is every bit as catty as you might imagine from movies like *Miss Congeniality*. Is the insincerity as thick as the hair spray? I would see girls try to undermine each other by getting inside their victim's head. Here's how it goes: Get to know a girl who you fear might beat you. Be nice to her. Encourage her to cling. Then say something undermining like, "Tracy, you look so beautiful, do you really want to do *that* to your hair?" This was a game I didn't play myself. But my years of experience with basketball helped me to instantly recognize these tactics when I saw them.

If the cattiness and artificiality were the downside, there were upsides too. We were sent to do a "buddy walk" with developmentally disabled youth. The itinerary instructed us to dress comfortably. I had done many similar events with Special Olympics, so I showed up in what I thought was appropriate: my Adidas sweats—the ones I used to wear for warm-ups before basketball games—a hat, and my red Converse sneakers. But even here some of the girls tried to outdo each other. Some of then showed up in six-inch heels with their hair all done up. I remembered how I had felt out of place when I'd worn the cocktail dress to the children's hospital—apparently these girls felt differently. Still, as far as I was concerned, they could have showed up in their swimsuits. I focused on enjoying the event—my favorite event of the entire three weeks I was in Las Vegas—and getting to know my buddy, a wonderful girl named Amanda, who reminded me, as if I needed reminding, of just how terrific it is to be able to work with disabled children. In a society like ours that puts such value on looks and intelligence and how much money you can make, it's good to be reminded that our humanity doesn't depend on our physical abilities, or whether we're the smartest, or how productive we are. Humanity goes a lot deeper than that. Every single child, from the most gifted and talented to the most severely disabled, is a unique and valuable human soul—and we should cherish every one.

While I loved this event and was thrilled that the Miss USA organizers had put it together, I nevertheless was having second thoughts. I had no intention of pulling out of the competition, but I knew why I had not wanted to compete again in the first place. I felt myself getting irritated with the whole pageant atmosphere, the insincerity of it all; and though I thrive on competition, this sort of competition had begun to lose its charm for me. Again, it was a matter of contrasts— fake hair, fake tans, and fake smiles were nothing to the sincere, beaming smiles of a disabled kid. I knew which was more rewarding for me.

Easter came, and for the first time in my life, I wasn't able to be in church on the most important day in the Christian calendar. I had asked my house mom if I could leave the hotel to go church, but she kindly said no. Later, I heard that some of the girls were getting together for Bible study. I hoped to join them, but the meeting fell through. So I read my Bible in my room, alone.

When word got around that I had been reading the Bible in my room, a number of the girls came up to me to talk about their faith. To be frank, I was surprised that no one made fun of me—maybe I had been too influenced by what Shanna had said about keeping quiet about God because the subject made people uncomfortable. Instead, I was awed by the strong, deep faith some of these girls expressed. I learned an important lesson in not to leaping to judgment. Far from being walking Barbie dolls, some of these girls showed maturity and depth, growing in their faith, wanting to help others, and hoping the pageant would help them do that work. To my mind, they had the right idea.

What you might not realize about the Miss USA Pageant is that there is a whole preliminary competition that goes on before the televised event. During this phase, I faced a panel of six preliminary judges for the swimsuit, gown, and interview events. These judges were regular people who wanted to get to know me. They asked me about my life, my school, and my hobbies. I tried to be natural, but of course I was standing tall above them on a stage. The judges looked at my contestant information sheet and saw that I volunteered at the Special Olympics. They asked me what I thought about Barack Obama's recent comments on the Special Olympics. President Obama had been on the *Tonight Show* with Jay Leno and made a comment about how his bowling skills were like something out of the Special Olympics. It was widely regarded as a bad joke. I said I had been disappointed by his remarks, because they could be seen as mocking the Special Olympics (or the Special Olympians themselves), but the president had apologized, and all of us make mistakes; and I reaffirmed my own passionate commitment to the good work done by the Special Olympics. As I watched the judges, it seemed to me they already had their favorites, their short list of candidates they thought would make it to the final cuts. I came out hoping I might be one of them.

One day after rehearsals, we finally got to meet Donald Trump, who, along with NBC, owns the Miss USA and Miss Universe Pageants. We were told to put on our opening number outfits—they were nearly as revealing as our swimsuits—and line up for him on stage. Donald Trump walked out with his entourage and inspected us closer than any general ever inspected a platoon. He would stop in front of a girl, look her up and down, and say, "Hmmm." Then he would go on and do the same thing to the next girl. He took notes in a little pad as he went along.

After he did this, Trump said, "Okay. I want all the girls to come forward." We stepped forward in unison, like soldiers asked to volunteer for a dangerous mission.

Donald Trump looked at Miss Alabama.

"Come here," he said.

She took one more step forward.

"Tell me, who's the most beautiful woman here?"

Miss Alabama's eyes swam around.

"Besides me?" she said. "Uh, I like Arkansas. She's sweet."

"I don't care if she's sweet," Donald Trump said. "Is she *hot*?

Miss Alabama shrugged, not sure how to answer. "Yes?"

He called up Miss Arkansas, and asked her the same thing. In this way, Donald Trump made his way through all the girls. As he did, he motioned those girls he liked over to one side, leaving the discards to one side of the stage. I was one of the survivors. Then he stopped, stood, looked us over, and smiled. It became clear that the point of the whole exercise was for him to divide the room between girls he personally found attractive and those he did not.

Many of the girls found this exercise humiliating. Some of the girls were sobbing backstage after he left, devastated to have failed even before the competition really began to impress "The Donald." Most of us respected Donald Trump as an amazing businessman and leader—and certainly I still do. But we naturally felt sorry for the girls who were left in the "reject" line. Even those of us who were among the chosen couldn't feel very good about it—it was as though we had been stripped bare.

Having survived the preliminary competitions—the official ones, not just the Donald Trump division of the hot from the not—I steeled myself for the big event, the national audience, the blinding lights, the cameras, and everything else that goes into the Miss USA Pageant. This was it—this was where the long nights in the gym, the two-a-day workouts, the study questions I had prepared for myself, and all the other training I had done would pay off if I won; and I was confident not only that I could win, but that I would make California proud, that I could bring the crown home to our state. As the announcers cried out their opening lines and the music swelled, I looked out from the stage and saw our ultimate panel of judges for the first time.

I expected that our judges in the televised show would be athletes and TV celebrities who could help with the ratings of this NBC event. Earlier that week, I had heard a rumor that Paris Hilton was going to be a judge. What would Paris Hilton ask me? Did I have a Chihuahua? All the girls were talking about this. What has Paris Hilton done that would make her an appropriate judge for Miss USA?

We were given an ice-breaker question so that we could get to know the panel a little and they could get to know us. Mine was about basketball. No question could have been easier for me—in fact, I can happily say, it was a slam dunk! During a commercial break one of the makeup artists told me, "It's going to be you!" But with all that good news, there was some worrying news too. Paris Hilton was not a judge after all. The judge was a man. His name is Mario Armando Lavandeira. He styles himself "Perez Hilton," "queen of all media," and he blogs about celebrities. His specialty is crude, child-like, superimposed drawings—usually a hand-drawn male sex organ—over the mouths of people he doesn't like. It took awhile to absorb this information: we were going to be judged by a purveyor of Hollywood sleaze. I couldn't help wondering if he had been using his internet skills to dredge up unflattering information about all of us, organized in individual computerized files. We found out that another judge was Holly Madison, a *Playboy* model and formerly Hugh Hefner's main girlfriend in a reality TV show. She had no pageant experience that I knew of, and I'm sure I wasn't alone in thinking that a woman who was "famous" for being a member of an elderly man's harem was not the best sort of judge for a girl to represent Miss USA. But con- testants don't get to choose their judges. An MSNBC reporter was a judge, and I thought that was okay—NBC was in partnership with Mr. Trump and the Miss USA organization. Two other judges were Claudia Jordan, a former Miss Rhode Island, and Kelly Monaco of *Dancing with the Stars* fame. Eric Trump, Donald Trump's son, was a judge too.

As one of the top fifteen contestants—six of us personally picked by Donald Trump—I first went into the swimsuit competition. It always feels a little creepy walking across a stage with just enough fabric to be legal. I did it and survived. That narrowed us down to ten girls. Next, we had to model our evening gowns. That brought us down now to five girls, and I was still in.

We entered the question round. I listened closely as other contest- ants answered their questions, trying to gauge what might be asked of me.

Some of the questions were tough. For example, Miss North Carolina, Kristen Dalton, was asked about bank bailouts. She answered the question with finesse. Miss Arizona was asked about healthcare. She described it as a matter of integrity. Her answer was really a non-answer—a bit too politically correct to carry any real weight.

In giving answers to pageant questions, Pam Wilson had always taught me never to forget where I came from. "Always remember what your parents taught you," she said. "Relate it to who you are, to the scenarios in your life. Think about how it relates to you, what you would like to see. Don't be too judgmental. Take a side, but acknowledge and show respect for other people."

While driving to Las Vegas two weeks before, I had gone over about 500 questions with my Mom. I felt prepared for just about anything—and my confidence had soared after the first round warm-up question about my basketball scholarship. I had nailed it. I was set to nail it again.

I felt ready, I had worked hard to be ready, and when Billy Bush called me forward I walked across the stage brimming with anticipation. I reached into the fishbowl and pulled out the card with my questioner's name. My nerves jumped a bit, though, when Billy Bush announced my questioner would be Perez Hilton. It didn't help when Nadine Velasquez said, "Are we worried?" and Hilton answered, "You should be."

Then came his question. There was something about his body language that seemed to want to enforce agreement, as if there were no other choices. Outwardly, I was all smiles. Inside, I was all turmoil, instantly thinking, *Why me? Of all questions, why this one? How am I going to answer?*

I paused to gather myself. I looked directly at Perez Hilton, taking stock of his spiky blond hair and lime green jacket. Following Pam

Wilson's advice, I acknowledged him. I spoke about the rights of states to legalize it if they want to. In fact, I was well on my way to sounding pro-gay marriage, almost as if all the falsity around me was leading me to give a politically correct answer. But I knew what I believed, and I knew what I had to say, and I knew I was representing California, the state that had just passed Proposition 8. I finally had to answer for real. I said that I thought that marriage was between a man and a woman, and that was what I had been raised to believe. For a minute, time froze. I saw my parents, my relatives and friends, and my sister all in the audience. I saw Donald sitting right in the front row, and I asked myself, *How does this question relate to me? How do I really feel about this? Do not give in and give the "world peace" kind of answer, Carrie; tell the truth.* The longer I spoke, the more the basketball chick in me came out. I thought I finished really strong, and I smiled at Perez Hilton.

To dead silence.

I remember Perez looking at me, looking at the judges, and then looking away from us all. He wouldn't make eye contact with me, or even look in my vicinity, for the rest of the night. I remember going back into my row of girls and turning to Miss Kentucky and saying, "Oh my gosh, what did I just say?"

She spoke to me between the gritted teeth of a forced smile, "You did the right thing." I felt so grateful for those kind words.

Miss Utah also tried to cheer me up.

"Just smile and look pretty," she whispered.

Mercifully, we soon went to a commercial break. As soon as the break was announced, I saw Perez leap up and begin to speak to the other judges. The commercial was over and the time had come to pick a winner.

They got down to the last two, and to my astonishment I was still standing.

I held hands with Miss North Carolina. Then they said that the first runner-up was California. I gave my most gracious smile and did what every runner-up knows to do—get off the stage.

CHAPTER SIX

Was It Something I Said?

The other girls began to react to what had transpired between Perez and me as soon as the lights went down. Miss Vermont later told FOX News, "A lot of people were shocked. We were all kind of giving each other those eyes. We couldn't believe it."

As soon as I got back to the tent behind the stage to change, someone shouted, "California, *Access Hollywood* wants to interview you."

"Why me? I didn't win."

As I walked back and put my flowers down, I felt all eyes on me, which was strange because I wasn't the winner, but there was this sort of buzz in the air, and it seemed to be buzzing around me. Part of it was that many of the house moms, who looked after the girls at the pageant, were coming up to me and whispering that I did the right thing in standing up for traditional marriage; they told me they were proud of me. I appreciated their kind words, but really my primary thought, after the letdown of losing, was to get out of this tight gown, take off all my makeup, eat a cheeseburger, and just go home and recover from the stress and strain of the last three weeks—weeks in which I had not seen my family, except in the audience.

I also wanted to get to a private room, turn on a computer or TV, and see what I had said. When you give a response under so much pressure, your memory of your own words isn't terribly reliable. I really couldn't remember my full answer. While I thought I had answered honestly and well, I no longer felt sure, and I wanted to see the tape and judge my performance. Given the reaction from the judges, I worried that I might have said something that I had not meant to say. Was it possible that I had said something truly awful?

Billy Bush had came up to me and said, "I just want to thank you for standing up and giving an answer...you're the only one of the final five I thought who gave an answer." He told me he was on his twitter account, tweeting his support for me.

I thanked him.

Then I heard someone shout a warning at me.

"Watch out!" one of the studio aides yelled, "Someone's here to hurt you!" Several girls bunched up protectively around me. I was told a fight had broken out in the lobby after someone ripped a picture of me from one of my supporters and tore it to pieces.

As the fear from that moment subsided, I started to get angry at fate for letting me get that question of all questions. My confusion over my answer deepened, because I still couldn't really remember it. Had I gone on and rambled like a former contestant once did, earning herself eternal YouTube stardom?

Two of my earliest glamour photos.

At "the beach" with my sister Chrissy and brother Billy, and at the plate as a softball slugger.

RED HOTS

MVC
Sports Cards

CARRIE
PREJEAN

3RD BASE

'99

Sports have always been my passion—softball came first, but basketball soon dominated my life. In the bottom picture, that's my sister, number 24, shooting a free throw. I'm number 30, looking to grab the rebound.

With my mom as a softball star. I also ran high school track and did the long jump.

At grandpa's 85th birthday. He died six months later. He was like a second father to me.

He didnt' like to talk about it, but he was proud of his war service for which he won a Bronze Star, a Purple Heart, and three campaign medals among other awards.

Me with my dad's parents, Anita and Billy Jones, and family friend Martha Moore, at the grand opening of Belmont Village Senior Living.

Here I am with most of my extended family on my mom's side.

Here I am (standing, fourth from the left) with high school friends, teammates, and church friends for a "Jesus Luvs You" walk to raise money for victims of Multiple Sclerosis.

With Chrissy, mom, and dad at my first big win: Miss Greater San Diego Teen 2004.

With Miles McPherson, pastor of The Rock. The former San Diego Charger gave me the spiritual counsel, direction, and support I needed when I suddenly found myself the victim of a hate campaign.

With Major Garrett and my dad at the Radio and Television Correspondent's dinner in Washington, D.C., in June 2009.

With Sean Hannity (above) and getting the thumbs up from Donald Trump.

With mom, dad, and Roger Ailes, CEO of FOX News.

With actor John Voight at Move America Forward, raising money for the troops, just after I was fired as Miss California.

At KUSI-TV with Dan Plante and Sandra Maas.

Here I am with Andrew Brietbart at the "Troopathon" event I did at the Ronald Reagan Library right after I was fired as Miss California.

Winning Miss California started as a dream come true—it became a nightmare.

With Miss Maine, a fellow basketball player, in the Nevada desert during the Miss USA competition.

Working with special needs kids is one of my greatest joys.

With my Miss USA roommate, Miss Hawaii, getting ready for our Best Buddies walk with special needs kids.

Me hanging out with my friends with The Rock's "Love-Em-Up" ministry.

My friend Amanda, from the Best Buddies walk, gave me this bracelet.

I was so happy to be able to tour the massive aircraft carrier the USS *Ronald Reagan* in the company of Michael Reagan and my Air Force sister Chrissy. This was exactly the sort of event I thought I should be doing, but I had to fight—and get Donald Trump himself to intervene on my behalf—to get the Miss California pageant directors to agree.

Michael Reagan, me, my sister, and my mom enjoyed a nice lunch before going on the ship.

Me, Michael Reagan, and Lieutenant Ron Flanders, public affairs officer for the USS *Ronald Reagan*.

The Miss USA Pageant cast a far different spotlight on me than I ever expected. But I'm still standing and I'll never back down.
(Steve Marcus/Reuters/Corbis)

I looked around the tent. None of the production staff from NBC—people who had joked around with me before—said a word to me or even looked my way. Keith and Shanna were nowhere to be seen. People started packing up their things and leaving.

The evening, however, was far from over. After the televised event, Paula Shugart of the Miss Universe organization always holds a coronation ball. It is meant to be a celebration for all the contestants, not just a celebration for the winner; it's a way to mark this special evening in one's life, to say goodbye to friends, to get past the contest. As first-runner-up, I also felt I needed to go to show my respect for the winner, Kristen Dalton of North Carolina. I wanted to go to say goodbye to the girls I had lived with for three weeks, especially Aureana. I didn't want anyone to imagine I was a sore loser. My parents were with me, tickets in hand, when I received a text from Keith telling me not to come—*a lot of people are mad at you, I'm afraid of what might happen to you. You really shouldn't come.*

I later heard from a friend who had seen Keith and Shanna in the lobby. Just before they angrily stormed out of the building, Shanna announced, "We told her not to talk about God! We told her not to talk about her faith!" This astonished me. I suppose my faith informed my answer, but what else could I have said? And shouldn't my pageant directors have been defending me?

I asked again. "Is that what Shanna really said?" My friend said, "Yes."

Excluded from the final event of the evening, my parents and I wandered around the empty corridors of Planet Hollywood. Exiled from the coronation ball, we found our way to a fast food café in the hotel. While everyone else was partying and celebrating, the first runner-up was in a little plastic chair eating greasy hamburgers with her family and friends.

Looking back now, I realize I had been too timid. I had the tickets. I should have gone to the ball, head held high. I should never have let Keith talk me out of going. But I was still in shock. And again, I couldn't remember exactly what I had said. For about the millionth time that evening, I winced at the possibility that I had misspoken and said something so awful I wasn't welcome at the coronation ball. How else to explain the widespread reaction against me?

I needed to get away from all this drama and hear my answer. I went up to my room. Miss Hawaii had already packed up and gone. I searched YouTube and saw my name instantly pop up—all over the internet. With apprehension, I clicked on the video and listened to myself over and over again.

I weighed my words, I analyzed them from every angle I could imagine—and then I decided I hadn't said anything wrong. I had tried to give a balanced, fair, and honest answer. I had done nothing to offend, I had merely (and I thought politely) upheld the traditional definition of marriage agreed to by the majority of my fellow Californians, and certainly the majority of Americans. What, then, was all the fuss about?

Later, in an interview, Donald Trump said of my answer: "It probably did cost her the crown. In that, well, I don't know that. . . . But I assume Perez probably gave her a pretty low vote and that would have brought her average down." Former Miss Rhode Island Claudia Jordan saw a lesson-learned in my answer: "In pageants, just like in politics, it's probably best to give a neutral answer where you're not committed to one side or another, if you want to win."

Claudia Jordan also said the judges were "bothered" by my answer. In fact, Perez didn't just give me a low vote. He reportedly said he gave me a "zero" vote. That I could sustain a zero vote from one judge, and very low marks from others, and still come in as first-runner-up left me with no doubt about how much my answer had cost me. As if to drive home the point, another judge, former Miss Nevada Alicia Jacobs, wrote on her blog: "If I could have made her fifty-first runner-up, I would have."

In a blog item titled "Pretty is as Pretty Does," Jacobs offers a behind-the-scenes account of the thinking of the judges and pageant officials. Here is her reaction to me:

> As she continued to speak, I saw the crown move further & further away from her. When she finished, she looked strangely proud for a moment. Personally, I was STUNNED on several levels. First, how could this young woman NOT know her audience and judges? Let's not forget that the person asking the question is an openly gay man, at least two people on the judges panel are openly gay. Another judge has a sister in a gay marriage. Her very own state pageant director, KEITH LEWIS, is an openly gay man who has been a very generous benefactor of hers... in many ways. (Two ways in particular... if you get my drift??) Did I mention I was STUNNED?

Yes, Alicia, you did. And in case anyone didn't get her drift, the "two ways" are a reference to my breast implants.

The hatred was only beginning to pour.

Perez Hilton immediately posted a ranting video blog that ricocheted around the world: "She gave *the* worst answer in pageant history.... Miss California lost because she's a DUMB BITCH, okay?"

He said, "If that girl would have won Miss USA I would have gone up on stage, I s**t you not, I would have gone up on stage and snatched that tiara off her head and run out of the door and then I'd probably have been arrested. But you know what? So be it."

Later, Perez told MSNBC in an interview, "I don't apologize. . . . Over the course of the past twenty-four hours, the more I've thought about it, the more—you know what?—No, I'm going to stand by what I said just like she's standing by what she said. And I called her the B-word, and hey, I was thinking the C-word."

He didn't mean Christian, Californian, or Carrie.

Soon after that, Perez Hilton began to post sexually obscene, offensive drawings over photos of my face. And this is the mature "expert" selected to judge the character, poise, and beauty of young women competing for the title of Miss USA!

As shocking as all of this was, I was even more shocked that I was receiving no communications or support from my pageant directors. Hearing nothing from Keith and Shanna personally, I did come across their public statements of support . . . for Perez Hilton.

"As co-executive director of Miss CA USA and one of the leaders of the Miss CA family," Keith wrote to Perez Hilton, "I am personally saddened and hurt that Miss CA USA 2009 believes marriage rights belong only to a man and a woman."

He added: "Although I believe all religions should be able to ordain what unions they see fit, I do not believe our government should be able to discriminate against anyone. Religious beliefs have no place in politics in the Miss CA family."

When I later heard this statement, I remember scratching my head at the last part. Religious beliefs have no place in politics? But politics has a place in the Miss California "family"—as long as it is religion-free?

And since when was the Miss California pageant a "family"? That word was getting tossed around far too easily. I know what a family is, and it's not a beauty pageant, and Keith and Shanna were certainly not my father or my mother or anything close to that. When pageants and other groups appropriate the name of "family," you know they're abusing that word. Here they were using it to imply that they were loving and inclusive—so loving and inclusive that they were booting me out of the "family."

To his credit, Keith did explain to the media that I was often attended to by gay beauty experts, and that he knew me to be friendly to them and to him. True enough. I was grateful to get that out on the record.

Nevertheless, I still didn't hear from Keith or Shanna; they were too busy broadcasting apologies.

"I want to apologize to our sponsors," Shanna twittered. "Ms. Prejean's opinions are her own and do NOT stand for the Miss California family." But who said I was standing for the "Miss California family"? Perez asked for *my* opinion—and I gave him an honest and respectful answer. But apparently when you're asked your opinion in the Miss USA competition, the judges are not really interested in *your* opinion. They want you to give the politically correct answer they believe themselves. And the game is, if you believe differently, you lie, you do anything to appease the judge and win, even if it costs you your integrity. That wasn't a game I was going to play.

But at the time, I felt devastated. Something terrible had happened. My pageant directors had turned against me; I was the subject of a torrent of abuse on the internet; and I still could not see how I had done anything to merit such an outpouring of anger, hate, and apologies on my behalf. Was it really so offensive to say,

Well, I think it's great that Americans are able to choose one or the other. We live in a land that you can choose same-sex marriage or opposite marriage. And you know what, in my country, in my family, I think that I believe that marriage should be between a man and a woman, no offense to any-body out there. But that's how I was raised, and that's how I believe that it should be—between a man and a woman.

I went to bed really upset. I cried a little and fell into a deep, dreamless sleep.

As it turned out, I didn't need a wake-up call. At dawn, the phone started ringing nonstop. The first call was from Billy Bush. He was polite and asked me what I thought of the pageant and about the controversy, and I tried to respond calmly and diplomatically. More calls came, mostly from the media. I was beginning to sense how big a story my little answer had become. But I had to focus on more practical things, like getting home with all my stuff.

I had brought three weeks' worth of wardrobe, which I now had to get back home to San Diego somehow. I assumed the Miss California organization would help me with transportation and moving my wardrobe. I called Keith Lewis five times, but he wouldn't pick up. Finally, after I had left a couple of messages, I got a hold of him, and I said I needed a ride home.

"Keith, all my luggage is here," I said. "I need a ticket home."

"Carrie, I'm still very upset by what you said."

"I don't know what happened, Keith. Can we talk about this later? I just need a ride home."

He told me he would pay for my plane ticket but not my luggage. The bill for a wardrobe filling six huge suitcases would be by far the

Roger wanted me to reinforce the first part of my answer, and buck the whole question back to the right of states to regulate marriage. He wanted me to punt.

I got on the airplane and took my seat in first class, feeling out of place in my jeans and Ugg boots.

The pageant was Sunday night, this was late Monday morning, and in about eighteen hours I would be sitting across from Matt Lauer answering questions about the most controversial social issue of the day. Miss USA always gets interviewed a few days after she wins. I would actually be going on *Today* before her.

I took another look at Roger Neal's statement. It was the handiwork of a professional spinmeister, but I didn't like it. It was designed to deflect, not to address. It didn't sound like me.

Once we were airborne, I began to panic, quietly. I tried praying, but felt as if no one was listening.

Lord, what I am supposed to do? I thought of catching the next plane home. I wiped my eyes with the airline cocktail napkins, and I had a little meltdown. *Lord, what have I gotten myself into?*

greatest expense, money I just didn't have. Being a member of the Miss California "family" apparently didn't count for much, because no other contestant was treated this way. They were all professionally managed and sent on their way home with planning and care.

I looked to Pam for advice. After all, I was told that when Perez asked his question, she began to shake her head in astonishment. Unfortunately, a health emergency forced Pam to rush to see a family friend. I also understood that Pam was in a difficult position. She had always been a wonderful advocate to me, but as the person who runs the Miss Greater San Diego pageant, Pam needed to maintain a good relationship with Keith over the long term. She really wasn't in a position to take sides, if sides had to be taken.

Pam did, however, graciously arrange for Debbie Dodge and her husband, Skip, to drive my clothes home. For that, I was very thankful. She had (literally) lifted a huge weight off my shoulders. With my luggage off, I dressed casually in an old blouse, blue jeans, and Ugg boots. I caught a shuttle to take me to the airport, where I would go to San Diego and try to forget the last twenty-four hours. On the way to the airport, my cell phone rang. It was Paula Shugart, head of Miss Universe. I was taken aback. In the pageant world, this is like getting a call from the White House.

"Carrie, I am getting all these phone calls," she said. "Larry King wants to interview you; there is the *Today Show*, *Good Morning America*, all these shows." She added, "Keith has given you the 'okay' to go."

That's when I realized the magnitude of the tsunami that was about to hit me. I got another call from Roger Neal, Hollywood public relations honcho for Keith, just as I was about to step out of the shuttle. (Roger played a big role in getting Keith through the Christina Silva fiasco the year before.)

"You need to get on the next plane to New York," Roger said. "I need to talk to you about messaging." He already had me lined up to appear on the *Today Show*, MSNBC, *Access Hollywood*, and *Inside Edition*.

I told Roger I didn't want to go to New York. I had already sent all my clothes to San Diego. I had no makeup or makeup kit. I was in jeans and a sweatshirt.

"I'll take care of it," he said, offering me a clothing allowance. So I agreed to go to New York.

I asked the shuttle driver to take me back to Planet Hollywood. There is a mall nearby, and I needed to find some appropriate clothes quick. I ran through a clothing store, picked out a skirt, a cute top, and pair of shoes, and rushed back to a shuttle to take me to the airport to catch the next flight to New York, which Roger had booked for me. I was rattled as I talked to Roger after clearing airport security. My phone was almost out of power. I remember sitting on the airport floor charging my phone, all alone, about to board a plane to New York. I knew this was a flight that could change my life forever—and not necessarily for the best. I was in a national controversy I had never sought, never wanted, never dreamed of.

"Carrie, I need you to focus," Roger said. "I need you to remember this. Carrie, a lot of people are mad at you. Keith, Shanna, and the sponsors are all mad at you. Everybody's mad at you. So this is your opportunity to make it up to the gay community. I understand your point of view. Right now, you can't think of you, this is about saving the Miss California brand. Don't talk about Prop 8, don't talk about faith or God or anything." Part of saving the Miss California brand, he told me, was not ruining his daughter Chelsea's chances of winning Miss Teen USA. (She was Miss California Teen 2009.)

He emailed me some guidelines for my "messaging. This is what he told me to say:

I believe that every state should decide what's righ their state regarding same-sex marriage. R California a majority of voters upheld the definit riage as only between a man and a woman. licenses marriages. Each state has the right to set of who can get married. California is a diverse s the Miss California USA platforms is regardin state's diversity.

Regarding the insulting things Perez Hilton hurt by them, I stand by my reputation as he standing by his.

Dating Michael Phelps—Based on all this c don't know if I will be able to date anyone.

Regarding offensive questions—That qu offensive it doesn't deserve a [comment].

The fact that Keith Lewis is gay—My ques about gay people. My question dealt with same not same-sex couples. I have a lot of gay frien and respect.

Prop 8—I did not lobby for Proposition 8. T riage as I have been taught was defined betwee woman.

If you don't have an answer to a question- enough about the subject matter to get specific my own state and the struggles we just went th

CHAPTER SEVEN

A Wing and a Prayer

One of the businessmen in first class kept giving me funny looks. Finally, he had to say something.

"Young lady, why are you crying?"

I told him I had been in a beauty pageant and had given what I thought was a perfectly straightforward answer to a judge's question. Now all hell had broken loose, and I was on this flight to New York only because I had to face hostile questions from about a dozen TV shows, and all I wanted to do was go home.

His eyes lit up.

"I know you!" he said. "You were at the Miss USA!"

"Yes, I was."

"You're *that* girl."

I nodded.

"Good for you," he said.

Then I told him about the media interviews that had been set up for me. He asked if someone had prepared me for such a big event. I showed him the memo from Roger Neal.

He studied it carefully, and then handed me the memo and said, "How do you feel about this approach?"

"I'm just not comfortable saying all this. It's not me. It has an apologetic tone, but what do I have to apologize for?"

He introduced himself. His name was Sean. He asked me to elaborate on my opinion about marriage, and then he started arguing with me. At first, I was troubled—I wondered if Sean was a very opinionated man just looking for someone to argue with. Then I realized he was playing devil's advocate—he was toughening me up for my big day of media interviews.

Sean pushed back on every point I made.

After a while, he said, "Carrie, you convinced me. You did nothing wrong. Just go out there and be yourself."

I appreciated Sean's help. As we landed in New York late that night, however, I felt my sense of panic return. There was one bit of good news: my mother had gone ahead of me. She would be waiting for me at the hotel, a strong shoulder for me to lean on. I needed to find her. I also needed to recharge my cell phone (I hadn't been able to fully charge it before I got on the plane) so I could catch up on changes to the next day's schedule.

Now that I was in New York and half a day from appearing on practically every major news outlet in the country, the worry really set in. On the flight across the country, I kept reminding myself of a passage in 2 Timothy that says that "all who desire to live a godly life in Christ Jesus will be persecuted." I also remembered a passage shortly after that saying,

No one came to my support, but everyone deserted me. May it not be held against them. But the Lord stood at my side and gave me strength, so that through me the message might be fully proclaimed and all the Gentiles might hear it. And I was delivered from the lion's mouth. The Lord will rescue me from every evil attack, and will bring me safely to the heavenly kingdom.

I hoped so!

I prayed in the JFK terminal as I had never prayed before.

"Lord," I quietly asked, leaning against a wall with my eyes shut fast, "let me know if I am doing the right thing. Give me a sign."

My prayer completed, I looked for somewhere to plug in my phone and find out just how long a list of interviews I had for the next day. I searched for an outlet in the luggage area and found one in a dingy corner. Immediately, text and voice mail messages began rising like popcorn, filling screen after screen. One text message in particular stood out.

"This is Miles McPherson from The Rock Church. I will be in New York City 10:30 Monday night, landing at JFK. Call me girl, I'm proud of you."

I fell to my knees and said aloud, "Thank you, Jesus, thank you!" Of all the people in the world, God had sent me my pastor. I had been going to The Rock for four years and, while I had loved Miles's sermons, I had never talked to him one-on-one. Still, I had always deeply admired him. Miles was always encouraging us not to be lukewarm Christians, but to stand for something, to do something. People milling about the terminal gave me weird glances as I sobbed and prayed. "Another nut case in New York," they might have thought. But I didn't care.

As many times as I had heard Miles preach, I still was a bit in awe of him. Would he really see me? Support me? I finally got Miles on the phone around 2:00 a.m., as I was being driven to the hotel, and heard that deep, melodic voice I had heard so many times before from the pulpit. He knew who I was, that I attended his church, and what had happened.

By complete coincidence, Miles was in New York to attend a board meeting. He and his lovely wife Debbie were also looking forward to visiting relatives. He said he had time to see me before I went on to my battery of shows.

He asked me where I was staying, and we soon realized my hotel was only eleven blocks from his. He told me to call him again after I got to my hotel. I didn't get to my room until 3:00 a.m. He was not irritated to be called again. This time Miles asked me to run through what had happened. I told him about my concern at trying to mealy-mouth my way out of the controversy, as Roger and Keith wanted me to do. I told him about the advice Sean had given me.

We walked through the issue and my beliefs, point-by-point. Miles thought of every conceivable question the media might ask me.

He also asked me, "Are you willing to lose the Miss California crown? The people who are confronting you are vicious and will stop at nothing. Are you ready to pay that price?"

I said yes.

Our conversation shifted to my first media appearance.

"What time are they coming to get you?" he asked.

My limo was coming at 6:00 in the morning.

"Don't worry," he said. "I'm going to get a little sleep. I will be at your hotel at 5:30 tomorrow morning and then we will go to the *Today Show* together." Then he said words that reached to the quick of my soul.

"Carrie, I just trust you."

Like most Americans, Miles McPherson had caught my answer two days before on the top of the news. At first, he did not recognize me—a tribute to my dyed hair and makeup. In fact, Miles later told me that when he saw my answer on TV, he said to himself, "I wish she went to our church."

The next day, the flight Miles and Debbie were on to New York from the West Coast was diverted from JFK to suburban Newburgh Airport. While sitting on the tarmac, Miles checked his cell phone.

There was one message: "We have a situation at the church."

"Every time I see that," Miles later told me, "my heart stops."

He called the church and was told that it had to do with Miss California.

"I don't even know Miss California," Miles said.

"She goes to The Rock and she was told to go to New York to face the media," his assistant told him. "Someone called and asked us to pray for her."

Miles tracked the call to my friend, Juliana. She told Miles what had happened to me and how distraught I was. He was concerned for me, especially being a 21-year-old sent off alone to make so many appearances on national television on such a hot topic with so little preparation.

I couldn't have asked for a better friend or a pastor with a deeper connection to how a person's life can take a tortuous path. While playing for the Chargers, Miles had gotten deep into marijuana and cocaine. One day, after his second season—April 12, 1984—he just stopped doing drugs and other sinful activities he now labels as "drama."

Debbie, he said, was just "trying to get me to be a boyfriend." Miles had bigger ideas than that. He became her husband in September

1984. Miles started going to Bible study with teammates. When he wasn't in training, he ministered in prisons, in high schools, and at special Christian events. After helping a few teenagers work to overcome drug habits, Miles started a Bible study for troubled teens. Soon, Miles had as many as thirty kids making regular trips to his house for Bible study. Some were kids trying to get off crystal meth, others were trying to get themselves out of gangs.

Then something happened to Miles that he compares to my own recent career jolt. In April 1986, the Chargers cut him.

Like me as a pageant winner, Miles was not ready to give up on the path he was on.

"I had had my best games against the Denver Broncos," Miles says. "So I called up the Denver coach and told him I was a free agent. He said he'd love to try me out. He called back the next day, and said, 'It's the strangest thing; they won't let me sign you.' This was really bad news. Signing up someone is a light commitment to just take them to camp. And who better to bring to the Denver camp than a guy who was a Charger, a rival?"

And yet Miles was not wanted, even as a prospect.

"God was saying, 'I got something different for you,'" Miles said. "But I kept pursuing it. Finally, a general manager told me that it is time in your life to move on. At the time, I took it as very condescending. I was only twenty-six years old, and I didn't want to walk away."

With football season over, and his future in the NFL looking bleak, Miles started doing ministry full time. He went to his pastor and told him about all the kids meeting regularly in his house. But if he was going to be a full-time minister, he would have to be paid.

"How much do you need?" the pastor asked.

"I need $1,500 a month just to make my house payments," Miles said. It seemed to him like a reasonable offer. After all, as an NFL player, Miles had been making $9,000 a game.

The senior pastor offered Miles $500 a month—and he took it. From that humble start, Miles built his Rock.

Miles later told me that he was standing in his hotel room at around 3:00 a.m. next to his open suitcase, saying to himself, "I thought the Prop 8 drama was over. But she goes to the church, she's twenty-one, she's eleven blocks away, okay God, what do you want me to do? It took five minutes to get there."

Sheer nerves kept me from feeling sleepy after only an hour and a half of sleep. I came down to the lobby at 5:30 in the morning and there, true to his word, sat Miles McPherson in a corner of the room, the lamp above his head—I swear, it looked like this—creating a slight halo effect.

The instant I saw him, I felt better. I sat down next to Miles. We prayed. He read a couple of Bible verses.

Miles looked at me and asked again, "Are you ready to lose the crown of Miss California? Are you willing to let it go?"

I said yes.

The limo came. We were taken to Rockefeller Plaza and escorted into the *Today Show* studio. Matt Lauer dropped by, said good morning in a friendly way that really bucked me up, and I thought, "Maybe this won't be so bad after all."

It was a tremendous comfort to have my mother with me. She sat with Miles in the studio behind the cameras while I sat on a couch under the studio lights for forty-five minutes. Every so often, the camera would cut to me while Matt Lauer added a promotional teaser—"Coming up, an interview with Miss California."

To my surprise, Kathy Lee Gifford herself came up to shake my hand as I waited to go on television.

The instant the interview began, I felt a sense of peace wash over me. Matt Lauer asked me about "the Question."

"You know what, Matt," I answered, "when I was on that stage that night and I was so excited to be there. I was competing for Miss USA, and I was called into the top ten and into the top five. I was standing, and I was ready for my question, and when I heard it from him, I knew at that moment, after I'd answered the question, I knew I was not going to win because of my answer."

"Because you had spoken from your heart?"

"Because I had spoken from my heart, from my beliefs, and for my God."

He then asked if I were given a do-over and was asked the very same question, would I answer it differently if it meant I could win the crown.

"No," I said, "I wouldn't have answered it differently....It's not about being politically correct; for me, it was being biblically correct....I know now that I can go out and speak to young people about standing up for what you believe in and never compromising anything—for anyone or anything, even if it's the crown of Miss USA."

Matt was professional and respectful. We got along well, and I considered the *Today Show* interview a success. On that program I got to explain my position in a calm, orderly way, to explain how I truly felt and what my intent had been. But that interview was only the beginning. A battery of interviews followed. I had a friendly reception at

FOX News, but an interview on MSNBC was rocky, bordering on snarky. I didn't expect that, because NBC is the network that shows the Miss USA pageant. Given how professional Matt Lauer had been, I expected the same sort of treatment from MSNBC, but I couldn't have been more wrong. Where the *Today Show* had been respectful but probing, MSNBC was openly hostile. Still, especially after the *Today Show* appearance, and as I did more and more interviews, I felt my confidence growing. I felt steady on my feet.

Miles was confident in me. If he had pushed my bike along with his prayers and support, now I was riding on my own. He wished me well and left to visit his daughter. My mother stayed by my side, however, and later my dad stepped in to help me, too. This controversy did not go away with a few television interviews. In many ways, it just seemed to grow and grow. But through it all, my parents really stepped up and supported me—something for which I am truly grateful.

While things were calming down on the East Coast, the West Coast was detonating.

In the middle of my interviews, I noticed that calls had been coming in from Roger Neal. He had been trying to get hold of me ever since 4:00 a.m., Pacific Time, when he got up early to see how I did on the *Today Show*.

We finally got in touch. Roger was furious with me for not sticking with his script. The Miss California pageant had been falling over itself apologizing for me, and I was not apologizing at all. We had two different messages, mine, standing by my answer to Perez Hilton, and Keith's, expressing his being "saddened" by my remarks. I told Roger

that if asked, I would address Keith's statement about being saddened. I told him flatly that I didn't appreciate being treated as if I had
made some kind of bigoted statement. Roger said something very
rude. I hung up on him. Roger then called my mom. He called
reporters and stations where I was doing interviews to lobby them to
cancel. Of course, his trying to stifle me with the press only piqued
their interest—maybe Roger wasn't such a clever professional spinmeister after all.

I told an NBC producer of the *Today Show* what had happened. He
smiled. "Don't worry," he said. "I'll set up everything." And he did,
helping me restore interview appointments. I went on and finished
my round of interviews. When I finished with MSNBC and once again
refused the option of walking back from my position, Roger Neal
called again. This time he was berserk. Before, he had just been
cussing mad. Now he screamed so loud my phone felt as if it would
jump out of my hands.

"You lost all of the sponsors! The sponsors are all gay, now they're
gone! The sponsors are hair and nail companies; they all had at least
one gay person!"

The final word I got from Roger was, "We're done with you...you
are on your own."

He made it clear I could book and pay for my own flight home.

At that moment, Shanna started Twittering, "I agree with Perez
Hilton 100%." She wasn't referring to gay marriage; she had already
made her approval of gay marriage as clear as day. No, she was apparently agreeing with Perez Hilton for calling me a "bitch" and a "c**t"
(the most degrading word you can call a woman). If the Miss
California pageant was a "family," it was surely a foul-mouthed one,
given the treatment I was receiving from Roger and Shanna.

Despite the provocations, the calm with which I'd gone into the *Today Show* interview stayed with me. When an interviewer asked me about Perez Hilton's comments, obviously hoping I would get upset or angry, I was able to deflate him and tell the truth I believed in my heart. I calmly replied that I would pray for Perez Hilton. And I do. I feel sorry for him.

Miles screened some of my phone calls that day and helped me figure out how to juggle all of the media requests that were coming in. I joked with Miles that he had become my personal press secretary. He gave me a look that I think a quarterback or two had regretted seeing. Little did I know that Miles would soon actually help me as a press advisor, keeping me from prematurely discussing a conversation that I would have with Donald Trump.

The next day I was set to see Mr. Trump at his office. Mom, Miles, and Miles's wife Debbie went with me to the big, brassy entrance of the Trump Tower. I was shocked to see paparazzi waiting, snapping photos, and yelling at me. *Access Hollywood* and *Inside Edition* were both there, right up front. They filmed me getting out of my car for the meeting with Donald Trump as if I were a head of state arriving for a summit meeting instead of a beauty queen in a PR disaster.

Miles helped us push our way through. Someone whispered, "Look at the bodyguard she's got!" I got a big laugh out of that.

My heart was racing as we walked through the pink-and-white marble, the brass and mirrors of the Trump Tower lobby. Donald Trump's office is ultra modern, but fairly modest for what you might expect. It is mid-way up his building, which was a surprise—I thought his office would be at the top of the world with a view of several states. But he is nothing if not a smart businessman. I guess it's better to rent out the upper floors. The office was large and messy, in a pleasant, busy way. The walls were covered with photographs of former Miss USA winners, sports stars, as well as family snapshots. I felt comfortable there, which surprised me, considering I was sitting in the office of the most powerful business man in the world!

Miles and his wife sat next to me, with my mother directly in front of Trump's desk. Mr. Trump greeted me warmly.

"I wanted to meet you," he said. "Carrie, you are fantastic, and you did not do anything wrong."

I felt a twinge of joy at those soothing words.

"In fact," he said, "you said the same exact thing as the president." (When I later Googled "Obama," "marriage," and "man and a woman," I found that Barack Obama's answer was almost identical to my own, although he managed to work in opposition to Proposition 8.)

Donald motioned for me to sit. He sat behind his desk, his eyes narrowing as I described the events of the last two days. He was very nice. So comforting—he felt more like an uncle than a powerful tycoon.

Finally, my mom could not contain herself anymore.

"Who picked Perez Hilton as a judge?"

There was dead silence.

Then Trump bellowed, "Get Paula Shugart in here *now*!"

Paula appeared almost instantly, hurrying into the office with terror written all over her face.

"Who picked Perez Hilton to judge this contest?" Donald asked her sharply.

Paula stammered, "I did."

I have never seen my mother so angry. She turned to Paula, horrified. "You picked Perez Hilton to be a judge of my daughter?" she asked in disbelief.

"He is controversial," Paula answered, adding that they needed someone provocative and interesting to update the pageant. "He has a pop culture image," she said.

Mom turned to Donald. "She should be fired!"

Sure, it's understandable that the pageant wanted a judge with a pop culture image. But Perez Hilton?

The Beatles have a pop culture image. Perez Hilton—a grown man who scribbles obscenities about people he doesn't like—has a problem.

My mother insisted that allowing Hilton to be a judge was only putting him in a position to exploit young women whom the pageant should have been protecting.

"He's exploiting them for money," she said. "Everybody's greedy, it's all about money."

All this talk about Perez Hilton seemed to agitate Donald Trump. He walked out to his hallway and barked at his staffers, asking if any of them knew who Perez Hilton was. After that, the meeting took a cordial turn. It ended with more warm words and a call by Donald Trump to his friend Regis Philbin. Trump thought Philbin might want me on his show, but unfortunately that never panned out.

Trump smiled at me as I was leaving and said, "I think this is going to be the best thing for you." He added that nobody knew who the new Miss USA was, but everyone knew who I was. (I wasn't sure that was a good thing.)

As I made my way out of the office, leaving Paula alone with Donald Trump, I could see the concern on her face. She saw, perhaps for the first time, that my family and I were serious and angry over how I was being treated.

Back in the lobby, the paparazzi were waiting, asking me how my meeting with "the Donald" had gone. I started to run over to them when Miles put his hand on my arm. Irritated, I elbowed him to get to the press. He grabbed my other elbow. When Miles McPherson wants you to stop, you stop.

"That was a private meeting you just had," he said. "The only thing you're going to say is that it went great."

When the reporters came over to me, I put on my brightest smile. They asked me how my meeting went. I said, "It went great."

All through the lobby, "It went great."

Into the car, "It went great."

Even now, I still think it went great.

Not so great was my relationship with Keith and Shanna. I felt as estranged from them as they surely felt from me. But we still had to get along for the seven months left in my term as Miss California.

As my critics (including the people I worked for) grew more vocal, I decided to become more candid. I set out to protect myself. And in America that means getting a lawyer. A great attorney, Charles LiMandri, began to research my legal options.

As a legal analyst told FOX News, I had grounds for a discrimination lawsuit.

"It's her religious beliefs which prompted her to say 'I don't believe in same-sex marriages,'" said analyst Mercedes Colwin. "So she was espousing her beliefs." She said I had reason to sue for violation of

Title VII of the 1964 Civil Rights Act, which prohibits discrimination based on religion. I wasn't thinking along those lines yet. But I was alarmed at how the Miss California Organization was treating me. I did want to know all my options.

To smooth out my working relationship with Keith (who would communicate with me only through tense emails), Charles LiMandri was invited to join a conference call with Keith shortly after the pageant. It was agreed in that call that I could appear wherever I wanted.

Conservative and religious-oriented groups were clamoring to hear me. So Keith allowed me to speak for them, as long as I didn't wear a sash and crown, appearing as Carrie Prejean, and not in my official capacity as Miss California.

Odd as it might sound, there was still a lurking possibility that if Miss USA winner Kristen Dalton went on to win Miss Universe in the Bahamas, I would, as first-runner-up, become Miss USA. In fact, it *had* happened before—to Shanna Moakler herself. If it had happened to me—now wouldn't that set the whole world on fire? This had to be working on Keith and Shanna.

All I could do was keep my head down and work. I continued my practice of filling in the holes in my schedule, only this time I was completely free to pick and choose my opportunities. Two weeks after the pageant, the Gospel Music Association asked me to go to Nashville to present the Dove Awards. I accepted. While on that stage in Nashville, I looked out at all the supportive people standing and applauding. I couldn't help but say, "Up in Hollywood, I'm not sure what their reaction would be to my showing up at a movie premiere." But in Nashville, they treated me like a heroine.

What was popular in Nashville, though, wasn't popular with the Miss California Organization. It didn't take long for the agreement

Charles LiMandri had reached with Keith over the phone to begin to fray and tear apart. I was asked to address 10,000 college students at Liberty University. When Keith agreed to it, I honestly think he didn't understand that the southern Virginia institution is a Christian college with a conservative character. True to our agreement, I didn't wear my sash and crown before the crowd. But Keith must have begun to realize the impact I was having on people as a result of my stance. To my surprise and horror, just as I was getting ready to appear, Keith threatened to file an injunction to keep me from speaking at Liberty.

"Can they do that?" I asked Miles on the phone.

"Whatever you decide to do, Carrie, always stand up for the truth, always stand firm in whatever it is that you believe," he said. "Don't be silenced."

And so I went out onto the stage and spoke to my fellow Christians.

I also took up an offer from Maggie Gallagher of the National Organization for Marriage to make a brief statement at the launch of their "No Offense" campaign at the National Press Club in Washington, D.C. Here are my remarks, as I wrote them out beforehand:

It's been a very strange week for me, as you can imagine. This was not exactly what I planned or asked for or wanted. But nonetheless I am grateful.

I'm grateful for all the prayers and well-wishes I've received from all different kinds of Americans who believe as I do that America is a place where people should stand up for our values, for what we think is right.

I'm grateful for the outpouring of support from the great majority of Americans who know in our hearts that

Americans should treat each other with respect even when we disagree—especially when we disagree about important moral issues like marriage.

You probably know by now, I believe very strongly that marriage is the union of a husband and wife. What's more, I believe with millions of other Americans: this vision of marriage is not hateful or discriminatory—*it's good.*

Marriage is good. There is something special about unions of husband and wives. Unless we bring men and women together, children will not have mothers and fathers. I do not want to raise my own children in a world where this traditional view of marriage is considered hateful or discriminatory, especially not by my own government.

I am not affiliated with any organization; I'm speaking my own views. But I do appreciate the many people who stand in the front lines to fight for marriage, including the National Organization for Marriage. That's why I agreed to appear today to support NOM's important message: Respect marriage. And the people who support it.

It's not about me, it's about the future of marriage. But I'm honored to do my part.

In introducing me, Maggie very helpfully made it clear that I spoke only for myself, not on behalf of Miss California.

While I was out of town, Keith Lewis and Shanna Moakler took the opportunity to shoot a "NoH8" (No Hate on 8) spot supporting same-sex marriage. Joining them were two other former beauty pageant winners—Miss California 2005 and Miss USA first runner-up in 2006 Tamiko Nash and 2008's Miss California Raquel Beezley. The spot was supposed to "raise awareness" to eventually overturn Proposition 8. The beauty queens wore their crowns, but had tape over their mouths and wrapped themselves in the American flag.

The Miss California organization put out the word that I refused to participate. In fact, they had scheduled the shoot for when they knew I would be out of town. The irony of the situation was not lost on me, either. It would have been all too appropriate for me to appear with a gag over my mouth. I certainly could agree with the central message of the ad, which said that no one should be silenced if they are speaking from the heart and with respect.

The NoH8 public service ad highlighted the dilemma I faced. It would be "too political" for me to appear as Miss California before Liberty University, but it was entirely appropriate and not at all "political" to parade recent Miss California winners—wearing their crowns and wrapped in the American flag—to denounce a state constitutional amendment a majority of Californians had just passed. No, that was not too "political."

Why did they do it?

"It's been a difficult time, but we want to show that there are a lot of different families," Keith explained about his ad. "I was raised by a single mom, and I am dad to two children that are being raised by two moms."

Shanna chimed in: "I believe Prop 8 [led] a campaign of confusion and never made clear what was being asked of the people. I find most people have a problem with the word marriage. What I hope for is helping others understand 'civil union' and then one day helping people learn 'marriage' is something not God, not the state or country can solidify, but between two people who love each other." Then she added, "If Carrie is going to go out there with her message, then we have to go out there and make sure the voices of these girls are heard."

Apparently I was not the only one asking why I was "political"—and they were not. Nor was I the only person who wondered whether marriage is just about "two people who love each other."

Shanna expressed a typical liberal view of marriage as nothing more than making formal the love between two people. This struck me as shallow. Maggie Gallagher put it far better than I could in a piece in *National Review.*

> Same-sex unions are really not just like opposite-sex unions when marriage is in question. Celebrating all forms of adult romantic love equally is not a very good justification for redefining a fundamental institution whose public purposes reach far beyond the affirmation of romance.
>
> Cultures that can no longer perceive anything special about unions of husband and wife will succumb to those that do. The future belongs to civilizations that commit substantial energy to generativity. Gay marriage is a bright red decision line: Once our government is committed to the idea that two men in a loving union are a marriage, there will be no retreat from that idea in the public square. Marriage will mean adults in love, not children in need.

It turns out that a lot of people were thinking the same way. A South Lake Tahoe fireman sent the following letter to Keith.

> Having enthusiastically watched many, many Miss USA and similar pageants over the years, we will from now on avoid any that you are associated with. You have shown astonishing lack of good judgment in your ridiculous comments about Carrie Prejean's answer, beliefs, and position about the gay

marriage issue so stupidly raised by that irrelevant goofball, Perez Hilton.

For your information, Mr. Keith, you are out of touch with the real world.

Ms. Prejean's position and beliefs are directly in line with those of a majority of Californians, as shown with Proposition 8.

Further, she has every right to her own beliefs and position, and right to articulate them, just as you have your own demented beliefs.

You owe an apology to Ms. Prejean, the Miss USA pageant, and to the citizens of California. We discussed this matter, and your lack of connect with reality, in our firehouse and 100 percent of the firemen and women are in complete agreement with this letter.

Columnist Ann Coulter, with her usual flair, wrote of me:

> She didn't even volunteer her "controversial" views on marriage. Rather, she was asked for her opinion on gay marriage and gave it—in an answer wrapped in so many layers of sugar it took ten minutes to get to the point . . . What a vicious hate-monger! Any second there I was expecting her to bust out a "by golly!" or an "oh my gosh!"

Truth be told, I'm not a "gosh" kinda girl. But I am grateful that most people saw the moderation and desire not to offend in my answer.

Here is a letter I received from California Congressman Duncan Hunter.

I am writing to express my support for your strong public statement in favor of traditional marriage during the Miss USA pageant.

As you have learned from your experience, standing firm in your beliefs can sometimes invite criticism from those who disagree with you. Please be assured that your unwavering commitment to your Christian beliefs is an inspiration to many. While the mainstream media makes it a common practice to discredit those who support traditional marriage, you have demonstrated how a person of character stands above the fray.

You now have a great opportunity as you finish out your reign as Miss California to continue speaking out in favor of conservative values. Through your work with Best Buddies and the Special Olympics you will be able to reach millions and show them that caring and compassion are the central tenets of your Christian faith. This has been evident in your interviews with the media as you have shown no malice towards those individuals who have been so critical and callous towards you for expressing your beliefs and exercising your First Amendment rights.

As you reflect on your experience, Mark 8:36 provides great solace: "For what does it profit a man to gain the whole world, and forfeit his soul?" You have stood for what you believe in and you should be proud. I wish you the best in your future endeavors.

I was grateful to know that there were so many people—in fact, most Americans—who either agreed with me, or who (including many who are gay) were incensed at the way I was being punished for giving a candid answer to a controversial question. Little did I know that the attack machine was just beginning its assault.

On May 1, 2009, Keith forwarded a message to his team and copied me. I got the same copied message from his boyfriend, Steven Kay, who wrote to Keith: "Sorry baby, a friend sent me this on Facebook...."

It was a petition to "dethrone Miss California" for "using her crown in a new crusade against a minority group." Because Miss California "must be of good health and moral character," the petitioners concluded, "Prejean is no longer an appropriate representative of the people of California" or ambassador for the state. It was sent to a long list of people, from Paula Shugart to Pam Wilson to K2 Productions to studios throughout the San Fernando Valley and California.

The real target was my morale. I instantly recognized this as trash talk, an attempt to "get inside my head." They wanted me to shut up and disappear. They wanted to put tape over my mouth. They wouldn't succeed.

CHAPTER EIGHT

Calling Donald Trump

I thought I had been through the worst.

But it was really just the beginning. Little did I know that I would soon face multiple lines of attack on my character, not only from media figures, but from my own organization.

The first line began when Keith and company continued to be as unhelpful as they could be on my scheduling. Ironically, they turned that around and portrayed me as a lazy prima donna who wouldn't meet even the most basic obligations of being Miss California. I worked as hard as I could to operate within the system, but they were determined to ensure it didn't work. The bottom line was that I wanted to be Miss California, I wanted to do what I thought that entailed, I wanted to represent my state in ways that helped other people, especially children, the sick, and those with disabilities. I thought Miss California should be an ambassaor of her state. But Keith and Shanna plainly no longer wanted me to be Miss California and were determined to undercut me at every turn. In retaliation for appearing with the National Organization for Marriage, for example, Keith put out a message intended to cut me to the quick.

"We are deeply saddened that Carrie Prejean has forgotten her platform of the Special Olympics, her commitment to all Californians, and solidified her legacy as one that goes beyond the right to voice her beliefs and instead reveals her opportunistic agenda."

It hurt, because my involvement with working with developmentally disabled youth preceded my time as Miss California—in fact, I was always fighting to get Special Olympics on to the Miss California agenda. Keith often delayed my work with the Special Olympics, holding out for "more details." Now they were accusing me of abandoning the one cause that is most dear to me. Besides, the Special Olympics had been my own platform, not an officially designated one. Contestants in the Miss America Pageant have platforms—but those in Miss USA do not. Obviously Keith knew that. Why was he speaking out about my supposed "platform" now?

The truth is, I had stayed true to the Special Olympics despite having to swim upstream against Keith's organization that placed no value on my appearances at such events. Watching them twist my love of the Special Olympics against me was mind-boggling. Around this time, Keith leaked some of my emails to him to the media. Some of them, written on the go, under time pressure and often after Keith had done something to provoke me, played all too easily into the organization's portrayal of me as hard to get along with; what was missing was the context—if I was occasionally sarcastic, it was because I was tired of Keith's playing games, and I was determined to make appearances where I thought I could do some good.

But there was an even larger context, of course: I was frustrated that my own organization—a beauty pageant no less—was using attack politics against *their own* beauty queen. It seemed unreal at the time. At some moments, it still does. I was asking for no special favors, and I was willing to play by the rules. But it was disconcerting, to say the least, to be Miss California and to be constantly, intentionally attacked, put down, and repudiated by the Miss California pageant, and all because I had, under direct questioning by a Hollywood sleaze merchant, given voice to the majority opinion of my fellow Californians. That was my "speech crime," and it seemed the Miss California pageant was determined to try to humiliate me for it. The press conference I did with the National Organization for Marriage had only increased their venom.

I checked with Charles LiMandri, who confirmed that Keith and his lawyer had agreed that I could make public appearances, specifically including the National Organization for Marriage press conference on April 30, in a private capacity as long as I did not use the Miss California USA title or wear my crown and sash. From the start, Keith and Company knew I was at the National Organization for Marriage press conference (where I was not, in fact, a spokesperson)—and approved it, but clearly Keith was suffering from a serious case of buyer's remorse, which he took out on me by leaking information that he thought would be damaging and manufacturing charges that I missed events. He had wanted to own me because I represented "his brand." Now when he found out he didn't own me— and he no longer wanted me because of my suddenly "political" profile—he was doing everything he could to discredit me; and there were many in the press who were happy to play up his charges without investigating them.

The allegation that I missed events was, in some ways, the most infuriating, given my long-standing frustration with the pageant on this very point. In essence, Keith used the Hollywood News Calendar that they sent me in order to make this accusation—the calendar sent, as usual, without asking me to do anything with it—and then accused me of missing all the events that were listed. By this sleight of hand, I was supposed to have missed thirty-two offers in one day, including, as my lawyer noted, "six events in a two and one-half hour period on May 19." I would have to have been cloned to have appeared at them all. So it was all a set-up, driven by accusatory press releases from the Miss California organization and founded on nothing.

On the other hand, requests for my time—one for an interview from an East Coast Christian radio station, another for an appearance from a Christian ministry headed by Stephen Baldwin—were flatly turned down by Keith. By this point I had become very frustrated, so I emailed Keith, asking him to forward all media requests to me. "Stop speaking for me," I said. "I have my own voice."

I made sure to let the world know that I was not sitting off on a beach somewhere, sipping piña coladas. Later, I told Matt Lauer, from the beginning, even prior to the Miss USA Pageant, I had taken it upon myself to book appropriate events. I called hospitals and different charities, and I said, "Hey, I'm Miss California. Would you like me to attend your event?" I hadn't missed a single event that had actually been scheduled. But Keith kept repeating the charge, hoping it would stick and deflect attention from suspicions that he might be attacking me for political or religious reasons.

As I grappled with this assault on my integrity, my employers made an even more personal attack—and in the process, I believe, violated laws protecting medical privacy—by revealing that I had had breast implants. On *Access Hollywood*, Billy Bush asked Shanna about my breast implants, and she confirmed it. Of course, a question like that doesn't just come out of the blue.

Nowhere did Shanna betray a sense that she was violating the privacy of another woman. She went so far as to join the show hosts in speculating on my new breast size, joking with them about my implants. And she made certain to tell the press, "I don't personally have them." Thanks for sharing.

Keith also made sure the message got out. He told CBS's *The Early Show*, "We assisted when Carrie came to us and voiced the interest in having the procedure done."

This was not true. The surgery was *their* idea, and they paid for it.

Nevertheless, this disclosure set me up for another round of attacks from left-wing talk show host Keith Olbermann on MSNBC who said I had been "outed" for breast implants, as if it were somehow hypocritical for a Christian woman to have such surgery. Carrie Prejean, he said, is "not just a boob, but a fake boob," who believes marriage is "marriage between a man and a woman who is partially made out of plastic." Appearing with Olbermann was *Village Voice* columnist Michael Musto. He predicted that I would someday be "looking for a husband who wants the only virgin in the world with breast implants." He called me "dumb and twisted." He also called me a "human Klaus Barbie doll"—in other words, he compared me to a Nazi war criminal.

Musto's parting shot was a bizarre bit about me being a homophobic transgendered man, who had been married several times (as a man), and who had the pageant pay to "cut off her penis."

There's no way I'm the only one who thought Olbermann and Musto came across like a couple of obnoxious, bullying, unprofessional punks. There is something unmanly about that kind of behavior. I wonder if they would say it to my face—not that that would make it any better, but it does seem pretty cowardly for them to broadcast denigrating jokes about a young woman, like two degenerate boys in a locker room; and I wonder how funny they would think themselves if I happened to be sitting across from them. And I wonder what their audience would think if they performed their Perez Hilton routine right in front of me. I know "reality TV" today is all about humiliating people, but I think there's enough residual decency in America that Olbermann and Musto might be exposed for what they are. It wasn't a one-off attack either. On a separate appearance on Olbermann's show, Musto dismissed me as one of many "bigotry-spouting women trying to cure cancer in bikinis."

What is this? Somehow the liberal media can get away with these degrading, disgusting jokes about a conservative woman, while still touting themselves as open-minded and tolerant. What if Sean Hannity or some other conservative media figure (male or female) had said something like this? Especially if he said it about a liberal woman? But for some reason it was perfectly acceptable for these men to belittle me on live television. Laura Ingraham pointed out the one-sidedness of "tolerance" in her television debate with Gloria Feldt (a liberal feminist who said I—another woman!—needed a "heart transplant" instead of breast implants). Laura commented—quite rightly—that she would be taken off the air if she spoke of liberals the way these media figures were speaking about me.

My parents were reeling. But no one was more upset than my sister. Liberal feminist that she is, she was appalled at seeing some of the most powerful news organizations in the world attack her 21-year-old sister like that.

It wasn't long before the implants story began to appear in the tabloids in snarky pieces like *The Star's* "Knifestyles of the Rich and Famous." I remember reading the piece and shaking my head. If I was famous, it is not a kind of fame I ever sought or wanted. And rich? I was having a hard time scraping together enough money to keep my cell phone account. Modeling jobs had already started to taper off and eventually stopped altogether. I did work for the San Diego Padres, but my schedule had become so hectic that I could only fit in a few hours here and there. Money was—to say the least—tight. I was a college student and beauty queen, not a lottery winner.

The attack campaign kicked up to a new level when they began dishing out every bit of dirt they could find about me and my past— two heaping spoonfuls of it.

The first one was a photo taken by a girlfriend of mine when I was seventeen. Taken from the back, it showed a generous amount of my skin, while not showing anything that would break a decency law. The picture had been made as part of a young model's portfolio. Someone, however, had photo-shopped it to take it just over the line, and it became an internet sensation. It was soon joined by another photo.

In early May 2009, I heard that an old picture of me was coming out. It was said to be shameful, ugly, unbelievable, and disqualifying for a Miss California. I braced myself, not sure what was coming. I should have known.

Here's the back story. In February 2007, after Keith's debacle with Christina Silva left me first runner-up, Keith signed me up with a Los Angeles modeling agency.

A photo shoot was arranged at the home of a famous photographer, Dominic Petruzzi, for *Blisss* magazine, an ultra-hip journal with lots of art, fashion, and surfing. I would be the model for the February issue of *Blisss*. I had heard about Petruzzi before, and knew him to be a top-of-the-line photographer, who had worked with big-name models. I saw this as a great opportunity to advance my modeling career, and was excited to work with him. While I sat in a chair for Dominic's makeup artist to work some magic, Dominic told me we would be going to the beach to do the shoot. He then showed me last month's model, and asked me to do the same.

"Dominic," I said, "she's naked."

He shrugged as if to say, "and your problem is?"

"I need a bikini top."

"We don't have any bikini tops here."

"I don't feel comfortable with this; it's not okay; I need to be covered."

Dominic thought a minute, fished around, and came up with a little cotton vest for me to wear. I asked him what I would wear underneath. The short answer was nothing. So I wore a bikini bottom and a vest.

And so off we went to a nearby beach. Dominic led me to a place where rocky boulders ended at a cliff. The cold winter wind cut right through me. It was so cold, in fact, that every five minutes or so I had to a take a break just to huddle in a towel we'd brought with us. I was worried about twisting an ankle on the rocks, or even worse—it would be entirely possible where I was standing to fall over the cliff and into the sea. Throughout the whole shoot, I struggled against the sea breeze to keep my footing while maintaining some semblance of modesty. Of course, in retrospect, I should not have allowed myself to be there at all.

But I did. And that mistake gave my detractors the ammunition they needed to launch a fresh round of attacks.

Out of the many pictures Dominic took of me, there is one from the contact sheets in which you can see most of my left nipple. Out of dozens of pictures he took, he chose to release that very one only after I had become embroiled in controversy. You can see why he did not pick this picture for *Blisss*. In it, the wind is blowing in my face. My face is half-obscured by my right hand as I try to rake my hair off my face. My eyes are squinting in the sun. But who cares if it's a bad picture. It shows part of a nipple, right?

I remember that after he took it, being a naïve new model, I said, "Oh my gosh, did you just get that shot?" He laughed at my reaction and said, "Carrie, I'm going to throw out dozens of these." I'm told Dominic might have been paid as much as $10,000 for releasing that picture.

When the press asked about the photo, I pointed out that the image was snapped at a vulnerable moment as I was standing on a rocky ledge above the Pacific Ocean in a high wind. I didn't know that I had been quite so exposed. This was portrayed as "Carrie blaming it all on the wind." No, actually, I blame it all on Carrie Prejean. No one put a gun to my head and made me do the photo shoot. But the truth is, I did not mean to show so much of myself. I was not taking nude photos. I was taken advantage of by a shameless photographer out to make an extra buck.

This was enough ammunition to spur a fresh round of attacks from Keith and Shanna. After all, I should have disclosed the infamous vest picture when I signed up for Miss California. They were shocked—

shocked!—by the photo. But they shouldn't have been. I had nothing to hide about this photo shoot—in fact, the actual *Blisss* magazine shot (not the wind-blown one I had been assured would be thrown away) was my main photo in my modeling portfolio. And it was funny watching Shanna, of whom every square inch can be seen with a click on any computer in the world, suddenly get a case of the vapors.

After all, if I wanted to take naked photos, I would have followed her example and posed for *Playboy*. Not only could I have done this, that's just what Keith suggested I do.

A few weeks after the pageant, Keith had called me and said that he had an offer for me.

One was for a reality TV show, "I'm a Celebrity...Get Me out of Here." It specializes in putting people in situations in which they cry, vomit, beg, and scream. I said, "No thanks, I'm not interested in reality TV right now." That certainly wasn't on my mind at this point.

Then he sent me an email with an offer to pose for *Playboy*. This was just after I had been burned for the vest photo. At the same time, Keith was declining, sometimes without my knowledge, offers to book me on Christian radio stations. He had no time for Christian radio. But he had plenty of time to forward on to me an offer to do a spread in *Playboy*.

He didn't directly advocate that I do it. But if I did do it, Keith let me know, there would be $120,000 in it for me, the shots would be limited to partial nudity, and I'd get to pick the photos.

When confronted by FOX News, Keith said that he did not ask me pose for *Playboy*, but was simply following my explicit request to be notified of all offers. He then released an email from me to the press, in which I requested him to forward all interview requests to me. I'd like to set the record straight here. He emailed me about the *Playboy* photoshoot on May 15 (two days after the press conference). I did not ask him to forward all requests to me until May 29—two weeks later.

"I know how you are and it's not right if you are selecting things for me," I said in the message to Keith. Perhaps he thought he was being clever. Perhaps he thought I'd jump at the chance for $120,000. Then he could be rid of me for good. Either that or the cultural gulf between us was so great that he saw nothing offensive about *Playboy* but plenty that was offensive about Christian radio.

I tried to contact Keith and Shanna to discuss the two modeling photos, but they would not return my calls. When asked on my pageant application if I had been photographed nude or in inappropriate publications, I had disclosed to the pageant officials that there was only one professional photo session I had been a part of, and that a variety of shots had been taken. No one blinked; it was absolutely true; and I had no reason to assume that an "I'm going to throw out dozens of these" photo, done by a prominent, legitimate, professional photographer (recommended by Keith) would suddenly become public, or even that it still existed. Considering that the co-director of the pageant had allowed her every asset to be photographed by *Playboy* and then posted on the internet, I found it hard to believe that anything I had done, even, as in the one shot, inadvertently, was over the line.

As if on cue, Keith Olbermann chimed in for his "WTF" moment to denounce my "amazing, holier-than-thou, know-it-all-ism" and hypocrisy.

"God and Satan, battling it out for the future of freedom of speech inside the head of St. Carrie of La Jolla," he said. "Where exactly were God and Satan when the Miss California people came to you and offered to pay for you to alter your God-given body with breast implants?"

Later, Olbermann said of the photos that it must have been "some kind of wind" that momentarily exposed me—"Satan's wind." Then he twisted the knife: "Your grandfather fought against that kind of wind at the Battle of the Bulge."

Throughout this controversy, I tried to accept comments like this as challenges to my Christian spirit, as invitations for me to live up to my principles, and in each and every instance I tried to love and forgive. But for the life of me, it is hard to overlook the viciousness of a 50-year-old with his own national television show attacking a college student who, by the way, is personally paying off her own student loans, and who has financial struggles like everyone else.

During one conference call, Keith Lewis apparently forgot that some of the people working with me had been invited to participate. He referenced the *Playboy* request and said, "For everyone's information, I would never let her do *Playboy*, but I have to offer it so when they take her title away she doesn't sue me." I don't believe he actually thought I would sue him for not forwarding on to me an opportunity to be in *Playboy*. Keith had inadvertently let it slip that he planned to fire me, and that everything that had happened to date was to publicly position me for that firing.

So far, however, nothing they had thrown at me—the boob job (which they urged on me and paid for), or the old photos (which struck many people as no big deal; in fact, Donald Trump later said he found them "fine and lovely"), was enough to get rid of me. These were designed to soften up my public image so they could then soak me with the main charge: missing appearances.

This line of attack was the killer. I had, it was said, missed more than fifty-three appearances in one month. The press went for it. When someone makes such a specific charge, the person being attacked is always at a disadvantage. It takes time to find out exactly what your accusers are talking about. By the time you do your homework and prepare to answer the charge, the damage is done. When I looked into it, these "appearances" were, again, really just the same old Hollywood News Calendar.

There were, of course, several events I declined because of scheduling conflicts or because they were designed to make me eat crow in public. One was an invitation from Keith to a mid-May event to attend the premier of a Hollywood docudrama promoting "same-sex marriage." Keith told me I could even go incognito by wearing a hat. He said I would gain credibility on the subject if the next day he could make a public statement that Miss California had attended a gay movie documentary.

I told him thanks, but I would take a pass on that one.

An event on which we did agree was my appearance at a jewelers' convention in Las Vegas. Although my contract did not permit Keith to take a fee for my appearances, he asked for a $500 cut of my earnings. Later, not wanting to be in breach of contract, he did return the money. At the time he requested it, though, I decided to let him have it to keep the peace.

Some peace!

Around that time, I asked Keith if I could visit the USS *Ronald Reagan*. Michael Reagan had called me himself, told me how proud he was of me and how much he supported me, and then invited me on the USS *Ronald Reagan* for my birthday! The ship was in port in San Diego with 5,000 sailors and Marines on board. I thought it would be an honor to go aboard the ship, a great way to show my support for the troops, and the perfect event for a Miss California—representing the state aboard a ship named after our former governor, not to mention president of the United States.

But Keith would not get back to me with a definite answer. He kept telling me to wait until he could get more details. "I'll let you know," was all he would tell me.

Finally, as the event drew closer and I still could not get Keith to decide, I grew so exasperated that I got in touch with Donald Trump. This was not the first time I had had to contact Trump to get Keith to allow me to attend an event. Donald was always available to talk to me, and I appreciated his support, especially since I knew it annoyed him to be bothered with our trivial concerns, when he had so many other things to worry about.

Donald took my side and called Keith on the spot.

"Why won't you let her go?" he asked. It was ridiculous, he said, to make such a big deal out of this. There was no reason I shouldn't go, and in fact it would be a lot of really good publicity for the Miss California Organization, and a good way to show support for our troops.

Keith had no real answer, and he agreed to let me go. I got a phone call from him shortly after that. "Carrie, you go," he said to me.

And so I did, on a beautiful day off the coast of San Diego. What a thrill it was to be surrounded by so many dedicated men and women in the military on the huge deck of this awesome, powerful carrier. I am so glad Donald Trump took my side on this. Because he was so decisive, I enjoyed one of the most memorable days of my life. Mom and Chrissy were able to join me, and we had lunch with Michael Reagan, who told us fascinating stories about his father.

Donald Trump also set up a chance for me to co-host *FOX & Friends*. At first, I felt tremendous pressure at being on national television and learning in real time to read from a teleprompter. But by the end of my time in front of the camera, I was having fun.

Despite the fact that the FOX opportunity had been offered to me by Donald Trump, Keith Lewis didn't miss a chance to make it look like I was being disobedient.

He told Radaronline.com, "We did not know about Carrie hosting *FOX & Friends* on May 27th. She did not ask if she could host the show, and, once again, Carrie is not in compliance with her Miss California USA contract and obligations."

I couldn't believe it. Was it possible there was so little communication within the organization that Keith did not know that Donald Trump himself had set this up? This just proved to me the distant relationship Keith had with his boss.

The most underhanded trick was a press conference at the Peninsula Hotel in Beverly Hills during which Keith and Shanna, feigning sadness, told the press that because I was not handling my responsibilities, they had to ask my first runner-up, Tami Farrell, to fulfill some of my duties as "Beauty of California Ambassador" to pick up the slack. After months of lackadaisical interest in events, Keith suddenly seemed to have a packed schedule of events that were going begging for lack of attention from Miss California.

Tami was naturally eager to step in. Earlier, she had told *Access Hollywood*, "I would be honored to represent the State of California if they need me for my responsibilities as first runner-up. I wouldn't mind stepping into the spotlight."

Keith told the press that my answer to Perez Hilton had not cost me the Miss USA title. I "was not winning" when I was asked that question, and, anyway, my answer lacked "edge." (I thought the problem might be that it had too much edge!)

Shanna, still fanning herself over the shock of the vest photo, said that I had entered the contest under "false pretenses." She also reiterated that I was often unavailable for important events for sponsors. (I didn't know that the Hollywood News Calendar was a sponsor!)

And why, the press asked, wasn't I there at the Peninsula Hotel to celebrate the appointment of the Beauty Ambassador?

Keith looked around, at a momentary loss. I had been invited, he said. But who knows why Carrie does what she does? All Keith could say was, "I believe she's, uh, en route to the airport to head to New York." As if I might be going to catch a Broadway show.

The reason I was not at the press conference is that I had not been invited to be at the press conference. The first I heard of it was when a reporter asked me to comment on it a few days in advance. I told him I had no idea what he was talking about. Larry Ross, my publicist, confronted Keith over the phone about this. This was the second time in about a week that Keith and Shanna had "scheduled" an appearance for me (the other was the pro-gay marriage public service ad) when in fact they had never invited me at all and knew I would be out of town—and then portrayed me as running out on them!

Keith was right about one thing. I was heading to the airport. I had been sent by the Miss Universe Organization to see Donald Trump, who was growing increasingly alarmed by what was happening in his organization.

The next morning in New York, Donald Trump's secretary called to say that our meeting had been pushed back an hour. When I got to Trump's office, I saw why. Keith and Shanna had taken the red-eye and were now sitting in front of a very angry Donald Trump. Even the windows seemed to be rattling.

Setting a professional tone, Donald said that we were all there for one reason—"to settle all this stuff" once and for all. The professionalism didn't last long. Shanna started yelling at me. I am sorry to say that I didn't hold back. I tore into Shanna for violating my privacy and releasing personal and medical information. While I spoke, Donald Trump nodded. He turned to Shanna, as you've seen him do on *The Apprentice*, and called her out on that.

Shanna didn't have a good answer. She hemmed and hawed and looked like she wanted to be in China. It was an awkward moment for her.

I then asked why they had not stood up for me against some of the more vicious attacks I had faced. Keith said what I said about gay marriage had hurt him. He said that I needed to get back to work. I replied that I would be glad to be Miss California, but I didn't feel I was getting any support. Moreover, thanks to the way the pageant had treated me, I now had reason to be worried about my personal safety, and I wanted the pageant to provide me with security for events. (Earlier, a gay British politician had said on live national television in the UK that I was a "silly bitch" and that he wanted to kill me. Another so-called "joke.") It was then agreed that I would get security.

Knowing that after our meeting there would be a press conference, I had written a script for any contingency. If I was to be publicly "fired" and humiliated, at the very least I wanted to explain myself, point by point. Hearing that I would retain my title, I crossed out the contentious stuff on the spot. Then I handed the script to Shanna.

"Look at this," I said. "This is all the stuff I was going to talk about. I'm willing to let it go." Shanna seemed genuinely touched that I had pulled back and was reaching out to her. She said some kind things to me. Both she and Keith thanked me.

Donald Trump seemed to like that. He agreed it was possible for us all to move forward.

I turned to Keith and said, "I've been through a lot. I want to be able to do speaking engagements as Carrie, not as Miss California. I want to be able to write a book."

In front of Donald Trump, Keith agreed. He only asked that I keep him informed of developments, and I said that I would. Then Donald walked me down to where the press conference was. Before the harsh lights and clicking cameras, he said that I had answered Perez Hilton's question just as Barack Obama and Hillary Clinton had done when they were running for president. He laughed off the embarrassing pictures of me, noting that we are now in the twenty-first century.

"Carrie," Donald declared in his strong voice, "will remain Miss California."

He went on to observe of Perez Hilton's question, "It was a controversial question. It was a tough question. It was probably a fair question, because it's asked of many people. And I've often said it, if her beauty wasn't so great, nobody really would have cared."

When Donald invited me to the podium, I began by thanking him for believing in me and allowing me to continue as Miss California USA. Trying to extend the good feelings from the meeting we'd just had, and, true to my word that I was willing to move on, I thanked the Miss California organization for their support "*thus forward*." (It was as gracious as I could be without being insincere.)

I turned to my script and again thanked the Miss California Organization for "believing in me, and believing in women; in the empowerment of women, and how women can really make a difference in the world." I added, "I would like to thank the Miss Universe Organization for allowing me to be here today. I would like to thank the thousands of Americans who have sent letters and emails. I cannot count the number of fan mail that I have received. They've confided in me that they have found hope and inspiration in my story. I would like to thank my Mom and Dad who are with me today. I would also like to thank my sister who is serving in the United States Air Force. And, most importantly, I would like to thank God for trusting me with this large task, and giving me the strength to stand by my beliefs."

And then I went on reading from this script I had prepared:

Three weeks ago, I was asked a politically charged question with a hidden personal agenda. And I answered my question honestly and sincerely from my heart. I was very careful to articulate in saying that I did not want to offend anybody, and say this is how I was raised. This is what I believe a marriage should be.

I stated my honest opinion, and as Mr. Trump said, the President of the United States believes that, as does the Secretary of State and many other Americans.

Immediately after the pageant, Judge Number eight started a cultural firestorm in the media. It went national. He was trying to be self-promoting and hateful, while I have remained silent, until I was honored to be here today. Now I can finally give my side of the story, and address the hateful acts, the false rumors, and the despicable acts that have happened over the last three weeks.

To be standing here today, representing the great state of California, and the greatest country in the world, is by the grace of God.

Being at the center of a media firestorm is not something that I had planned, or signed up for. But the days since have taught me to stand up for what I believe in, regardless of the consequences, personal attacks, or disagreements.

I am a strong woman, and because of that, I am able to be the best Miss California USA I can be. I am excited to continue my duties and represent California.

Let me be clear: I am not an activist. Nor do I have a personal agenda. I was thrown into this firestorm when I was asked the question. I have become an advocate for not redefining marriage based on my own upbringing and beliefs.

While I am not the most vocal proponent of traditional marriage, it seems that because of my singular response I have become the most visible.

I am proud to be an American. I am proud of the freedoms we enjoy because of the brave men and women serving this great country, and who have served. My grandfather served under General Patton in World War II and is someone I admire greatly. He never spoke of the Battle of the Bulge, in which he participated as a rifleman, or the honorary medals that he received. But he did speak of the freedoms that he fought for, and he taught me to never back down, and never let anyone take those freedoms away from you.

On April 19th on that stage I exercised my freedom of speech, and I was punished for doing so. This should not happen in America. It undermines the constitutional rights that my grandfather fought for.

I publicly forgave Perez Hilton and wished him the best. In the Q&A that came after our statements, Donald Trump was asked if he would have Perez Hilton back as a judge. Too clever to step into a trap, he said he would "love" to have him back as a judge. When asked about his personal view on gay marriage, Donald brushed it off. He simply said that the press conference "isn't about me."

When the press conference was over and we were in the elevator, Donald looked me in the eye and said, "Carrie, your speech was genius. I am really impressed!"

That was flattering, but I was even happier that, thanks to his support, this whole nightmare was behind me (or so I hoped), and I could go back to being Miss California, serving the people of my state.

The last thing I had said in our meeting was, "Wow, we really accomplished a lot today." A day later, I turned twenty-two, and it seemed as if my life had turned a corner. Then I heard that Shanna had given the whole controversy a new life by resigning in protest.

"I cannot with a clear conscience move forward supporting and promoting the Miss Universe Organization when I no longer believe in it or the contracts I signed committing myself as a youth," she said. "I want to be a role model for young women with high hopes of pageantry, but now feel it more important to be a role model for my children. I am sorry and hope I have not let any young supporters down but wish them the best of luck in fulfilling their dreams."

Keith Lewis responded: "Shanna has, and will continue to be, a large part of my life. Although I am sad she has come to this decision, I will always respect the convictions that brought her to this place."

On *Access Hollywood* and *Larry King Live*, Shanna—being the living role model that she is for young women—proceeded to attack me again for my photos. Appearing on *Access Hollywood* with Keith, Miss USA Pageant judge Alicia Jacobs, and Miss Universe Organization president Paula Shugart, Shanna said she resigned because I was being "rewarded for breaching" my contract. Paula tried to strike a nicer tone when she said that as of the day of the press conference, "it's a fresh start." Alicia Jacobs, who earlier had said that she wanted to make me fifty-first runner-up after my answer to Perez Hilton's question, got in a dig, saying she wished I had been "honest" about the photos.

On *Larry King Live*, Shanna restated her reasons for resigning. Donald Trump phoned in to the show and put her on the spot.

"I was a little surprised at Shanna," Donald Trump said.

Shanna visibly stiffened in her chair.

Why was he surprised?

"Because she was in my office, and she seemed as if everything was fine. And she was actually going at it pretty hot and heavy with Carrie"—meaning, in Trump-speak, that we were getting along—"and I was a little bit surprised she would deal with it that way."

Donald said he didn't know Shanna that well and was sorry she had handled her disagreement by resigning after making peace. Shanna then responded that in the press conference, I had pointed fingers at everyone else but had never taken responsibility for myself. Of all the vicious, mean, underhanded things Shanna Moakler has said about me—well, this time she had a fair point. I had put myself in a position to be exploited. I had signed myself over to the Miss California

Organization. But I was more innocent then than I am now. Keith Lewis and Shanna Moakler were not my friends.

"I can't go back to my state and run a healthy pageant when my contract means nothing," Shanna said.

After her slam on me—that I had, essentially, poisoned the entire Miss California Organization—a prominent columnist rallied to my defense. It was Ann Coulter—a conservative woman well used to the hostility of the liberal media and its harsh personal attacks. In her inimitable sarcastic style she wrote,

> First, the Miss USA contest held a press conference to announce that Prejean had breast implants. Take a Christian position in public and Satan's handmaidens will turn all your secrets into front-page news. Next, a photographer released a single cheesecake photo of Prejean. This prompted liberal reporters who have never met a Christian to proclaim that Christians were outraged by the photo.

Coulter surmised that liberals actually hate women and that the only way for a woman to succeed in the liberal media is to wear the burqa of liberal conformity.

> The only way to protect yourself is to do the liberal male's bidding, as the bubble-head anchorettes do, or stand on the rock of Christianity. Now, another beautiful Christian has thrown off the liberal burqa, thereby inciting mass hysteria throughout the liberal establishment. Prejean doesn't care. She is blazing across the sky, as impotent nose-pickers jockey for a piece of her reflected light by hurling insults at her.

Funny and encouraging words, but I still wanted to think that all the media attacks and the subversion from the Miss California organization were over; that some sort of normalcy would return to my role; that I could do the job I was crowned to do, which Donald Trump had affirmed that he wanted me to do—with the cooperation of the people who crowned me.

After all, how much worse could it get?

CHAPTER NINE

Fired by Radio

Not surprisingly, I began to feel push-back on the book deal. I guess Keith, who had hastily agreed to allow me to write a book in front of Donald Trump, was experiencing yet another case of buyer's remorse.

After many telephone calls, my lawyer sent Paula Shugart an email discussing how we could proceed with a book deal and how we could arrange my private speaking engagements. My mom and I actually had lunch with Donald Trump during which we discussed this issue. I told him I wanted to be able to do speaking arrangements in my private capacity (not as Miss California), and I told him I wanted to write a book. We agreed that what had happened to me was so unusual that it was worth setting down on paper.

After lunch, we went up to Donald Trump's office, and he asked me what I wanted to happen. I had a written agreement from my lawyer, I said, that I would like him, or at least Keith Lewis, to sign. He said he would, and then he yelled to his secretary to get Paula Shugart on the phone immediately. On speaker phone, he asked her if she had my lawyer's written agreement regarding speaking engagements and writing a book. She said she did. Donald said, "Make sure you get this thing signed, Paula, okay? Carrie just wants to write her book, she's not going to say anything bad about the Miss Universe Organization; she just wants to tell her story, and I think that's okay." After I left Donald Trump's office, I called my lawyer and Miles and told them about Donald's kind words and his promise that he would get the agreement signed.

Donald also went out of his way to help me again. He organized a meeting for me with *Star* magazine (including meeting its CEO) to clean up the malicious slander that my mother was a lesbian—by far, one of the most humorous attacks, considering my mother is one of the most womanly women I know. He also organized an interview for me with *Shape* magazine. The editor-in-chief of *Shape* magazine arranged for me to do an interview with shape.com. I ended up being part of a video called *Women Who Shape Our World* for their website. It was great. They came to San Diego to film me working out and eating healthy. Later, Keith said I had been in breach of contract by doing the interview with *Shape* magazine. Either the communication between the Miss Universe Organization and the Miss California Organization was amazingly bad, or Keith was just so desperate to find an excuse to fire me that he grasped at every straw he could find.

With Donald Trump's assurance that I could do a book, it seemed safe to accept preliminary inquiries from publishers. But before getting a serious bid through an agent, I wanted to have the supplemental clause to my Miss California contract signed, sealed, and delivered. Whether the signature was Donald's or Keith's or Paula's didn't matter to me, but I wanted to have it done. The organization, however, kept putting it off, so I called Donald and reminded him that Keith had agreed to it, and that I would like to have it signed so we could proceed. Paula got back to me to say that she was still working on it. Though Keith had agreed in principle, I suspect he was the sticking point. I kept hearing that Keith was beside himself, anguishing over what I might write about him. With Shanna now on the outside giving one interview after another, and Keith in a dither about the book deal, the pressure was back on Donald Trump, with him once again having to take time from his business empire to deal with our petty issues.

On June 10, 2009, I drove to an event to raise money to help low-income kids from San Diego's Barrio Logan neighborhood go to college. As I drove my Jetta, I talked into a speaker phone, being interviewed by Billy Bush on his national radio show. It was from him, an interviewer on live radio, that I learned I had been fired.

"We just found out from Keith Lewis, you know, your executive director there, that it's official, that they put out a statement that you have been fired."

I must have driven a hundred feet before I answered.

"Well, that's the first I've heard of that, Billy," I said, adding that at least that explained why I kept getting otherwise perplexing messages from so many people, but it contradicted my recent improved relationship with the pageant officials. "Everyone had been getting along so well. This is the first I've heard of it. I mean, this is funny to me. I have no idea what is going on."

Later, Billy Bush told Larry King, "I was shocked that she didn't know.... Some people would say maybe you should have contacted Carrie ahead of time and let her know this was coming."

After the interview was done, I still thought it might have been a joke or a rumor. Surely even Keith wouldn't buck Donald Trump who had brought us back together and publicly affirmed his faith in me. Moreover, I only had a few more months to go as Miss California. Even if Keith had come to despise me, or even fear me with the possibility of a book deal looming, presumably he could have tolerated me for just a little bit longer. But as my mind raced, I wondered if the Miss California Pageant's guerrilla war had continued, if they had worked at chipping away at Donald Trump's support. That frankly wouldn't have surprised me, because they had certainly seemed obsessed with meting out endless retribution for my answer to Perez Hilton's question. As soon as I could, I went to a computer and found a press release from K2 Productions, Keith's company.

I immediately called the Miss Universe Organization to find out what was going on. Right away I knew something was odd. Usually when I called Trump's office, I would be put through to him right away. This time, his secretary told me he was unavailable.

"What can I help you with?" she asked me.

So I asked her to fill me in.

She said she had no idea that I'd been fired, which made me suspicious. She agreed to make some calls and then get back to me with any information she could find out. When she did call back, all she could do was confirm that I had indeed been fired; she had no further specifics.

The only details, or fabrications, came in Keith Lewis's press release.

"This was a decision based solely on contract violations," Keith said in the release. "After our press conference in New York we had hoped we would be able to forge a better working relationship. However, since that time it has become abundantly clear that Carrie has no desire to fulfill her obligations under our contract and work together."

It was classic Keith, in his more-in-sadness-than-in-anger, passive-aggressive style.

The statement from Donald Trump was a little more stinging.

"I told Carrie she needed to get back to work and honor her contract with the Miss California Organization, and I gave her the opportunity to do so," he said. "Unfortunately it just doesn't look like it is going to happen, and I offered Keith my full support in making this decision."

Tami Farrell immediately stepped forward to claim the sash and crown—and those duties I had allegedly let slip. In fact, my supposed "missed appearances" had suddenly gained so much importance that Miss USA and Miss Universe were both called on to fill in as necessary, as the organization announced to the press.

At no time did anyone point an index finger at me and say, "Carrie, you're fired." Instead, I later received a letter from Keith's lawyer, "Re-Notice of Title Revocation." It had been given to the media with no advance warning to me or to my attorney. Keith didn't even have the guts to call me. Predictably, Perez Hilton was all set to crow over this one. "This is too funny!" he chortled in a blog titled, "Dumb Bitch Reacts to Being Fired." "Former Miss California, Carrie Prejean, is pretending not to know she was getting fired yesterday. That's like a bank robber that doesn't expect to get arrested! Dumb."

As Tami Farrell took over as Miss California, Shanna also saw a place for herself.

"First and foremost, my faith has been restored in the Miss Universe Organization and with Donald Trump," she said. "I believed eventually what I intimately knew would come to fruition." Intimately? I am sure she did have intimate knowledge that my firing would eventually come to fruition. She had apparently known it ever since I answered "the Question" the wrong way.

Later, Donald was quoted as saying, "Carrie is a beautiful young woman, and I wish her well as she pursues her other interests." TMZ reported that he also said, "To me, she was the sweetest thing. Everyone else—she treated like s**t."

Throughout it all, I have never blamed Donald Trump—and I still don't. Like many CEOs, he has to trust what his people are telling him. And he has to get along with people who are not mere employees, but who have ownership stakes in this part of his media empire.

Nevertheless, it was, of course, a devastating turn of events for me. My reign as Miss California was over. What was supposed to have been a dream come true—the climax of my ambitions as a beauty pageant competitor—had in fact been turned into one long nightmare. Though I know myself to be strong, that nightmare had taken its toll on me. I had lost sleep, been depressed and anxious, and been sub-jected to more personal abuse than I could have imagined—and through it all, my own pageant officials viciously undercut me, actively worked to betray me, and came to the aid of my enemies at every turn. Now they had dismissed me—wrongfully, not only as regards the facts, but in terms of their motivation, for I was obviously being fired for the expression of my religious beliefs, beliefs that I had not offered gratu-itously, but that had been solicited under direct questioning.

Still, as shocked, angry, and depressed as I was at what had happed, there was at least this consolation. Now maybe I could put all this behind me. While I had hoped to do great things as Miss California, to be an active public servant in my role, those hopes had been dashed, and if they weren't to be fulfilled then it would be a relief to be done with the sashes, the crowns, and all the other stuff that went with being Miss California. I could get back to being my normal, sports-crazy self.

Or so I thought. In fact, I was once again being naïve. My ordeal was far from over. The hate campaign would only intensify.

As I said before, I had been volunteering for the Special Olympics for years. I saw no conflict in continuing with them as plain old Carrie, even while I was still Miss California. Before I was fired, the Special Olympics contacted me, reaffirming that I would be appearing as a presenter of medals to the athletes at an event. I replied that I was looking forward to the event, and that I was excited and honored to be a part of it.

But I had made a big mistake. In a post-firing interview, I mentioned that I would be presenting at the Special Olympics over the weekend as an honorary guest. I had inadvertently given Keith yet another chance to pull the chair out from under me.

The Special Olympics people called me back. The Miss California Organization had scheduled Tami Farrell to make her first official appearance with Special Olympics. Keith specifically asked the organization if I would be presenting awards. When they said that I would, he demanded that I be uninvited. In the interest of the athletes, I didn't make a stink about it. They graciously offered to let me present awards the following year.

It was a completely petty move by Keith—all so phony, so classless, and so unnecessary. Tami is a fine girl, but she had no special connection with the Special Olympics. For Keith, the Special Olympics had always been one of those tiresome requests I was always bringing up to try to make Miss California a useful agent. Now that I was out of the picture, the Miss California Organization was suddenly clamoring to claim my passion.

Meanwhile, the intimidation campaign began to include a new dimension—legal threats. Keith's lawyers were firing off emails, each one backed up with threats to sue. As a college student with little money, I was terrified.

"Mr. LiMandri," Keith said in a statement, "obviously has never watched *The Apprentice* if he believes that Mr. Trump could be so easily fooled. Facts are facts and we stand by them. No matter what strong wind the General Council of the National Organization on Marriage will blow, our vest of truth will stay on." Uh, Keith, I think you meant "counsel," not council. And thanks for the snarky, ridiculous metaphor about the wind and the vest of truth.

I no longer had the slightest bit of respect for Keith, but Donald Trump was another matter. The Donald Trump I got to know is a little different from the hard-charging executive we see on *The Apprentice*. He is thoughtful, intelligent, and always adapting to the needs of the moment. Like any good businessman, he is not afraid to change his mind. And he is too smart to allow his many businesses to face the prospect of a boycott.

After I found out I was fired, I decided I needed to talk to him. I called Donald Trump on June 20. I wanted to hear it from the man himself.

We exchanged a few "how-are-you's,"and then I got right to the point. I said, "I'm confused: why *did* I get fired?"

"Carrie, you're a great girl, but you know Keith said you missed over seventeen appearances, and that you weren't cooperating. You guys just didn't get along, Carrie."

Of course, I had not missed those appearances. But I couldn't deny that Keith and I didn't get along. Still, I didn't think that was my doing.

I hadn't abandoned Keith when things got tough, he had abandoned me. I asked Donald about his comment, as it was quoted in the press, that I had treated him well but everyone else badly. He denied saying that: "No I said you were a good girl, but that you didn't get along with some people." By some people he meant Keith. Throughout the phone call I had the very clear impression that Donald knew very few of the details of what had actually been going on. He was obviously relying on Keith's testimony, and I had the strong sense that Donald had felt pressured into approving my being fired against his better judgment. I knew he had tried to help me in the past, and he reminded me that I had once noted that the pageant business was a small part of his life. He couldn't be on top of every little niggling problem in the organization.

He cleared his throat. "So Carrie, tell me something, why did you miss so many appearances?"

I asked him to remember how hard it was get anything on my schedule, even when *he* was forced to intervene. I didn't miss appearances; the problem was the reverse, I couldn't get the organization interested in them. Why was he firing me, I asked him, without even a list of "missed appearances?"

"I don't know... Carrie... I don't know. You just didn't get along."

But I wasn't going to let it end there.

"Did you see the list of appearances Keith says I missed?" I asked.

Donald said, "No."

I asked him point-blank: "Mr. Trump—you fired me without making sure you had all the facts?"

"Sorry, Carrie," he answered. He sounded uncomfortable. "I tried to help you, but Keith says you missed seventeen appearances. I can't have that. I have to support Keith's decision."

We ended our call on a friendly note. In the months since, Donald Trump and I have talked many times. He has been very supportive and encouraging. If there is a villain in this piece, it isn't Donald Trump. He operated based on the information he was given. It was the Miss California Organization that was relentless in its efforts to take me down.

Throughout this controversy, the Miss California Organization had to worry about a public backlash. I wanted to put the whole controversy behind me, but the organization couldn't; they had to keep proving that they were right and I was wrong, because, I believe, they feared that public opinion might be moving against them and in favor of me. Now they went to work to convince the press that I had never been given approval to move ahead with a book—even though it had been agreed to in principle. Moreover, up to the moment they fired me, the pageant organization had repeatedly reassured me that the supplemental contract, which would put that agreement in writing, would soon be signed and completed. Despite there being no book deal—at that time, there was no book, no manuscript, and no publisher—Keith's lawyer said that my "participation in the admitted book deal unquestionably violates the contract and appears to be a knowing and deliberate violation." I suppose that shows just how much Keith feared this book, or even the prospect of this book.

How do I feel about Keith now? There are times when I feel sorry for him. Beginning with the Christina Silva fiasco, Keith has made a wreck of the Miss California Pageant. There is no doubt that my answer caused him a problem with his sponsors, though I can't help but think that his attacks on me made things worse rather than better. Most of all, I couldn't help but feel that Keith failed to respond to the controversy with dignity and finesse. Instead, he seemed to prefer to rely on character assassination, leaking emails, and conspiring against me with charges that were incontestably untrue.

Keith went on *Larry King Live* after my firing to say that it wasn't any one thing I did wrong, but "many, many things." For example, Keith said, "She came to us and said, 'I'm not interested in your input; I'll make it my own decision what I'm going to do.' You know, when you have a contract, when you're working for someone, you have a responsibility to follow through on what that requirement is."

The take I gave Matt Lauer on my firing was, I believe, closer to the mark.

"I'm here talking to you because of the answer I gave on that stage," I told Matt. "It's a test to Americans' tolerance. Tolerance needs to be a two-way street, and it's not. This is about me stating my beliefs about same-sex marriage, and that's the reason why we're here today."

Keith's people still circulated the story that I was a prima donna who wouldn't go to events. They put out the word that I had missed "tens of tens" of appearances. But I thought I could put a stop to that by calling their bluff.

I asked Matt Lauer if Keith had specified any of the "tens and tens and tens of appearances" I had missed.

"No, he did not talk about that," Matt replied.

I pointed out the absurdity of the charge. Keith was accusing me of missing "tens and tens and tens" of events in a one-month period. How could I have possibly missed—take your pick, "fifty-three appearances" or "tens and tens and tens" of appearances in a single month?

After that round, after nailing the fact that they couldn't name a single event I had missed, I was foolish enough to breathe a sigh of relief. That was that. The story was over. They couldn't possibly continue that line of attack because they couldn't back it up. There were no facts behind the charge. Some people might enjoy media exposure, but I had had enough; I was tremendously looking forward to getting out of the public spotlight and having some private time, which I needed, to recover from this whole terrible experience. I wanted it to end.

Once again, though, it not only didn't end, it got worse. The next blow hit not just me, it hit my whole family.

Ann Coulter wrote:

> Finally (so far, anyway), reporters gleefully released the divorce records of Prejean's parents. Because when you want the truth, what is more reliable than angry accusations traded in the middle of an acrimonious divorce?

> Liberals used the divorce papers to argue that Prejean had some deep-seated psychological disturbance causing her to oppose gay marriage. Symptoms of this debilitating illness include a belief in some sort of 'god' and a reverence for the Bible.

Meanwhile, more of my heated emails to Keith were released to the public and got a lot of play on the internet. Hastily typed on a cell phone at gas stations and red lights, I had given Keith all the ammunition he needed to keep convincing members of the press that I was spoiled rotten. "Oh," chimed in an *Entertainment Weekly* blog, "what a tangled web we weave...when first we leave a big ole electronic trail of evidence showing that we are kind of a huge pain in the ass."

As a result, the blogger wrote, I was now a "new spokeswoman for opposite employment." (Kinda witty, that one. At least it had more class than Keith's "vest of truth.")

My lawyer fired off a message to Keith's lawyer condemning the portrayal of the Hollywood News Calendar as scheduled appearances.

"These were NOT requests for her appearance as your client has been repeatedly, falsely, publicly stating," he wrote. He continued:

> This is slander per se. The daily Hollywood News Calendar was no more a request for public appearances by Carrie than the Entertainment section of your own daily newspaper is a request for a public appearance by you. The chart that you sent us is basically a fraud as she was not declining specific requests for an appearance except for the three that I mentioned in my letter to you yesterday. How very shameful your client's conduct is turning out to be as the plot unfolds. No wonder Carrie lost her cool with him when he forced her to go to Mr. Trump directly just to get permission to greet the troops on the USS *Ronald Reagan* and the Special Olympics.

The organization's lawyers retaliated by trying to shut me up, just as they did in threatening an "injunction" to keep me from speaking at Liberty University.

"If Carrie Prejean wants to assert in public that she was courteous, cooperative, or professional in her conduct as Miss California USA, the history of her churlish, insolent misbehavior can be presented," Keith's lawyers wrote my attorney. "Instead, let me recommend that Ms. Prejean and her spokespersons acknowledge that her professed professional cooperation was nonexistent, recant the recent falsities, and avoid further public deviations from reality on the issue."

And if I didn't shut up immediately, if I persisted in telling my side of the story, I was threatened with "firm action."

Not everyone was in the thrall of Keith, his publicists, and his lawyers. The Alabama House of Representatives passed a resolution praising me for sticking to my convictions.

Others just opted to stay out of the way. I knew Tami Farrell held the same opinion as I do on same-sex marriage. After she became Miss California, however, she avoided the heart of the question, saying, "I don't think that I have the right or anybody has a right to tell somebody who they can or can't love. And I think that this is a civil rights issue. And I think that the right thing to do is let the voters decide."

There is nothing here to disagree with. Certainly it has never been my intention to tell people whom they could or could not love. If you look at it closely, this is a "non-answer" answer. I remember saying to the TV set, "You're a nice girl, Tami, but you wimped out."

I was resolved not to wimp out. I was confident that if I had to go to court to clear my name, I could prove that I had been treated unfairly. A great case could be made that I had been illegally punished for candidly answering a question put to me at an event set up by my employer that struck at my personal religious beliefs. Certainly, an airtight case could be made that my medical privacy had been violated. At one point in the summer, I thought that Keith's lawyers might concede all this, because it was so obvious. But in the end, nothing changed.

Looking back, I can see that I often gave in all too easily. Keith and Shanna wanted me to have breast implants, and I let them push me into it. They wanted me not to talk about my faith so much, and at times I soft-pedaled my beliefs. They kept from me from the coronation ball, so I didn't go.

But at some point I learned that standing up for myself was far more important than wiggling into the tight costume of someone else's idea of who I should be.

I hadn't answered "the Question" the way they wanted it answered.

I hadn't gone on the world media apology tour that they wanted.

I hadn't backed down for them.

I got angry, but I didn't let my anger warp me. I didn't let my abuse at the hands of Keith, Perez Hilton, and a few others turn me into an anti-gay bigot.

In retaliation, they had thrown everything they could at me.

They had dug into my past, my photos, my personal emails, my parents' divorce records. They had set up events without inviting me, only to portray me as a prima donna who fails to show up. They had fired me and called me every name in the book.

And yet, as I look back now, I do so with peace and contentment.

They gave me the greatest gift of all. They showed me who I really was and what I was really about. They helped me return to my core beliefs. Shanna had wanted me to stop talking about God. But in the end, I knew that if I had erred at all, it was in listening too much to people like Shanna and not enough to what really matters: the still, small voice of your own conscience. Being right with the Miss California Pageant is a lot less important than being right with God. For me, pageants had always been about competition and using that sash and tiara for good. Now I saw the whole pageant as a sham, glittering and fake. Many of the people I had worked with and the girls I competed with were wonderful. But we were trapped in a system run by petty egos, shallow values, and a sort of venomous incompetence. I was glad to be done with it, and I was only sorry that the pageant had fallen into such hands and that it might harm other young girls as it had harmed me.

CHAPTER TEN

Gagging Free Speech

I knew my Miss California experience would put me in touch with a lot of new places and faces. I never thought that it would involve me in the politics of the British Parliament. But it did, thanks to Alan Duncan, a leading figure in Great Britain's Tory Party. If the Tories win the next election, its leader—David Cameron—will, of course, become the Prime Minister. It is reported in the British press that Duncan, an openly gay man, is Cameron's choice to serve as Home Secretary, the official in charge of British police and security.

You might think Alan Duncan has enough on his mind. But in his busy schedule, he had time to take a break and comment on a beauty pageant in the United States for BBC1's *Have I Got News for You*.

After calling me "homophobic" and a "silly bitch," Mr. Duncan threatened to murder me.

"If you read that Ms. California was murdered, you will know it was me, won't you?" he said. One British internet news site reported that many viewers saw the comment as something you just don't say, like yelling "bomb" on an airplane.

Later, Duncan said his statement "was in jest." He said: "It is a comedy show after all. I'm sure Miss Prejean's very beautiful and that if we were to meet we would love each other. I have no plans to kill her. I'll send her a box of chocolates—unpoisoned."

Many times since Planet Hollywood, I have gone to search my Blackberry, worried about what I might find on the internet. The outpouring of abuse from bloggers, commentators, and others could seem at times almost overwhelming. This time I also had to wonder, "Where is Keith?" A man makes a public statement about murdering your Miss California, and you can't bring yourself to stand in front of her and protect her? Or was he about to issue another press release, this one saying, "I can fully understand why Mr. Alan Duncan would want to murder Carrie Prejean for her extremely homophobic remarks that have no place in the Miss California family. I apologize on Carrie's behalf and hope that Mr. Duncan will refrain from killing her."

When I looked up Alan Duncan online, I was a little reassured. I saw his apology. I also saw his picture. He is a dashing man in a well-made suit. If I ever go to London, I think I actually would like to meet him. Not only do I expect to be perfectly safe, I bet he would be a pleasant and witty person to get to know. I am sure we would, in fact, "love each other." But I'd also like to ask him a few questions.

You do know, don't you Mr. Duncan, that the answer I gave was the answer given by most of the people of my state, my fellow Californians, the entire United States? Do you feel the same way about them?

And do you really believe that our answer on marriage reveals us as fearful and even hateful towards gay people?

I'd also ask this well-educated Englishman what he thinks "homophobic" really means anyway, besides being a slur on anyone who opposes a politicized gay agenda.

If you ever get bored, look up "homo" in the dictionary: it means "man" as in Homo Sapiens or "the same" as in homogenous, so to be "homophobic" really means to be fearful of men, which I'm not, or fearful of things being the same, which is a fear I think few people have. "Homophobic" is merely a made-up word to try to force everyone to be politically correct on gay marriage or risk being accused of being hateful.

Perez Hilton even told the press, "Yes, I do expect Miss USA to be politically correct." Technically speaking, Perez could have been a bit more politically correct himself, considering Vermont's legislature—not its citizens—legalized same-sex marriage. His question never seemed to take that into account. Those of us in favor of traditional marriage might be in the majority, but it's an embattled majority; and the venom spat at us by the minority seems to be excused by the mainstream media in ways that would normally seem shocking. During the Proposition 8 campaign, proponents of gay marriage ran an ad that specifically targeted a religious denomination for abuse. The ad opened with two Mormon missionaries knocking on the door of an attractive lesbian couple and saying, "Hi, we're from the Church of Jesus Christ of Latter Day Saints." Then, "We're here to take away your rights." After they take the women's wedding rings and rip up their marriage license, the two Mormon men say: "That was too easy." "Yeah, what should we ban next?" Whoever thought we'd live to see the day when it was acceptable to target an ad against a religious group: Mormons this time, but maybe next time Jews or Catholics or

Evangelical Protestants. Political correctness seems to trump religious freedom.

The liberal media seems to encourage this alarming trend by finding it so unremarkable, or even by encouraging it. On a similar note, the media targets conservative women and makes them the focus of particularly harsh criticism. There seems to be something about conservative women that inflames the left and calls out the attack machine. I can only imagine it's because "women" are all, in the liberal media's eyes, supposed to be liberal feminists. And if they're not, then they are fair game to be demonized and attacked.

Think about Sarah Palin, a governor, a former vice presidential candidate, a woman who is beautiful, intelligent, a wonderful mother, and was relentlessly torn down by the liberal media. One extremely prominent gay columnist even fanned despicable gossip that Sarah Palin's Down Syndrome baby was not her own but was the baby of one of her daughters! The sort of catty, personal insults the liberal media hurled at Sarah Palin would rightly have sparked a firestorm of media criticism if they'd been hurled at someone like Sonia Sotomayor or Michelle Obama.

Palin became such a lightning rod that she's apparently going to enter the dictionary as a new word. The new word would be "Palinized"—which is what happens when conservative women enter public debate. They can expect to get Palinized by the liberal media. Michele Bachmann, an attractive, conservative congresswoman from Minnesota, has been getting just that treatment; she even sent out a letter to her supporters asking them not to let liberals "Palinize me." As Congresswoman Bachmann said, "With Governor Palin taking a well-deserved step out of the spotlight, it appears that I may be absorbing even more of the liberals' scorn." I know what that feels like.

On one particularly bad day, I got a surprising phone call that cheered me up no end: it was from Sarah Palin.

We talked for a good fifteen minutes. She told me that she was extremely proud of me and told me to stay strong.

"You tell it like you see it, Carrie. People are sick of politically correct answers. You're doing awesome."

I told her how brutal and vicious I thought the media attacks on me had been, and she said she completely understood, given her own experience.

There are few women I respect more than Sarah Palin, and I have to say this is probably the first time I have ever been star struck. She also was an amazing comfort to me. There are some things in life I've learned already, that no one can really understand unless they've been through it themselves. Well, Sarah Palin had been through the media shredder as I had been, and that made all the difference in how we understood each other. She was sympathetic and reassuring and told me that everything was going to work out. She gave me hope and courage to keep fighting the good fight. She told me her daughter Bristol was a big fan of mine, and would love for me to call her. We have been keeping in touch ever since.

I won't try to draw out lessons from Sarah Palin's experience (an experience shared by many other conservative women, such as Michele Bachmann, Elizabeth Hasselbeck—re-named "Elizab***h" by Perez Hilton in a post on his website—and Ann Coulter), but I can say that in my own case, I think my whole ordeal reveals just how the culture of political correctness uses shaming, blackmail, and other forms of emotional abuse to force people and organizations to either stick to our beliefs and suffer the consequences, or throw away our beliefs just to be left alone.

Not every form of coercion is social. Sometimes, it is legal.

When I was threatened with an "injunction" to keep me from speaking at Liberty University, I didn't know enough about the law to realize that Keith couldn't find any judge in America who would issue such a gag order. I now know that this kind of "prior restraint" is almost unheard of in America. But that didn't keep Keith's threat from sending a chill down my spine.

The real importance of what happened to me is what it shows about free speech in America. At the press conference with Donald Trump, I spoke of being punished for exercising my right to freedom of speech.

I said: "On April 19th on that stage I exercised my freedom of speech, and I was punished for doing so. This should not happen in America. It undermines the constitutional rights which my grandfather fought for."

Keith Olbermann and other liberals saw my statement as an opportunity to teach a thing or two about the U.S. Constitution to the dumb, blonde beauty contestant.

In one segment, Olbermann brought the First Amendment to a big screen. He read it aloud. It states that, "Congress shall make no law respecting an establishment of religion, or prohibiting the free exercise thereof; or abridging the freedom of speech, or of the press; or the right of the people peaceably to assemble, and to petition the Government for a redress of grievances."

Olbermann took me to task for not knowing that the First Amendment only protects my speech from the *government*. It doesn't, he said, protect my speech from opposition from others, or even from termination by my employers.

He's right about a lot here. The Miss California Organization had every right under the Constitution to make *their* opposing statement, even if it was against their own beauty queen. And even in America, we can be punished by others for our speech and associations. After all, employers have *their* right to free association. They can hire and fire at will.

I get that.

But Olbermann still misses the point.

I never said that my constitutional rights were violated. What I did say is that I was "punished" for my beliefs—which I clearly was—and that this "shouldn't happen in America" because it "undermines" the constitutional rights my grandfather fought to protect.

Of course, I always knew that I would be in front of the cameras and that I might be asked a controversial question. But if you ask me how I'd vote on a ballot issue, surely it is contrary to the American spirit— and as I said *undermines* my constitutional rights—to smoke out an ordinary political view and then punish me for it.

The Miss California and MSNBC organizations have a constitutional right to be as liberal as they want. But Keith Olbermann can't ask his cameraman on live TV how he votes, and then fire him for voting Republican, or fire him for voting from a Christian perspective. Isn't that why we have curtains at the ballot booth?

And another thing Olbermann should know. The constitutional rights of Christians *are* being violated. I didn't have to look very far to find a case in which a Christian is being defended by none other than one of Keith Olbermann's favorite organizations, the American Civil Liberties Union. In fact, I only had to look across the nearest freeway.

Poway is a San Diego suburb about a ten-minute drive from my aunt's house, where my mother and I are staying while I write this.

A young Christian, Tyler Chase Harper attended his local high school when the Poway Unified School District decided to stage a "Day of Silence" in April 2004. The idea was that students could voluntarily wear tape over their mouths and speak in class only through a designated teacher. This was supposed to demonstrate the "silencing effect" of intolerance of homosexuals in our society.

Tyler Harper is not the kind of guy to let anyone slap tape over his mouth. So in protest, he wore a hand-written T-shirt to school. On it he wrote, "Be ashamed, our school embraced what God has condemned." On the back of his shirt he wrote, "Romans 1:27"—referring to the passage the apostle Paul had written in which he condemned homosexual behavior.

Now, Mr. Olbermann, you may not like this. You may not believe it. But doesn't Tyler have a right to express his opinion?

Tyler's second-period teacher told him that his shirt was "inflammatory." (Somehow it was not "inflammatory" for a taxpayer-funded school to promote an agenda on homosexuality.) Tyler refused to remove the shirt and was sent to the school's office. An assistant principal told Tyler he could return to class, but only if he got another shirt or turned the one he was wearing inside out. Tyler refused.

Next, the Poway principal asked him to change his shirt. They told him his shirt would incite hate and psychologically damage other students.

Tyler refused.

So they called in the Sheriff.

Tyler was interrogated by a deputy sheriff to find out if he was a "dangerous" student. So while a few students paraded around wearing tape over their mouths—and the vast majority was cowed into silent submission—Tyler Harper was in the principal's office being treated like a terrorist.

Tyler's rights had been violated. And so he sued. When he filed a suit to protect his speech rights, who came to his defense? The ACLU of San Diego and Imperial Counties, which filed a friend of the court brief on his behalf.

The ACLU's David Blair-Loy told *The San Diego Union-Tribune* that this case marked a "novel and extreme expansion of a school's rights to limit speech."

What about the danger that Tyler's t-shirt would be psychologically damaging? Blair-Loy said: "And let's face it: what about high school is not psychologically damaging? This student wore a t-shirt that expressed an idea. It's an idea we don't agree with at the ACLU, but that is the essence of free speech. It's not just for ideas you like."

Robert Tyler, one of Harper's lawyers with the Alliance Defense Fund, said he saw a "double-standard" at work. He asked: "Why is it acceptable to tell a student of faith their views are not as valuable as the view of any person opposing them?" One appellate judge, Alex Kozinski, made a common-sense observation: "Harper's t-shirt was not an out-of-the-blue affront to fellow students who were minding their own business. Rather, Harper wore his t-shirt in response to the Day of Silence, a political activity that was sponsored or at the very least tolerated by school authorities."

As the lawsuit made its way through the courts, Tyler graduated and his sister, Kelsie, took his place as a plaintiff.

After a lot of legal wrangling, U.S. District Judge John Houston came down to a firm decision—on the side of the school. In early 2008, Judge Houston wrote that the school had an "interest in protecting homosexual students from harassment" and that this "is a legitimate pedagogical concern that allows a school to restrict speech expressing damaging statements about sexual orientation and limiting students to expressing their views in a positive manner."

What about protecting Christian students from legal harassment?

Non-believers are free to reject Romans 1:27. Liberal Christians can explain away Paul's denunciation of homosexuality. But Evangelical Christians will always take our guidance from Scripture, and traditional Catholics will always take their guidance from the teachings of the Church. And that view is, and forever will be, the one expressed by Tyler Harper. You may not like it. But are we really in a place now in America where we are ready to persecute tens of millions of Christians for expressing traditional beliefs?

There is talk that the case will go to the U.S. Supreme Court. It should, because the practice of persecuting traditional Christians for holding traditional beliefs is only spreading; you only have to read the newspaper with open eyes to see that. And you have to wonder, too, how it is that public schools, supported by taxpayer dollars, have taken it upon themselves to teach our children what to think about homosexuality. Isn't there another word for that: isn't it "indoctrination"? If it isn't right for the public schools to teach a single faith perspective, how can it be right for them to teach an anti-faith perspective, to teach that homosexuality is a normal lifestyle, when to faithful Catholics and Evangelicals and others who support traditional morality, it isn't? This sort of double-standard in our public life is dangerous, but it's what political correctness is doing to us: it is putting not just our freedom of speech, but our freedom of conscience at risk. How far are we from laws that would outlaw quoting certain passages of the Bible as hate speech? That's already happened in other countries, including our next door neighbor Canada. It's not hard to imagine it coming here.

In 2007, California Governor Arnold Schwarzenegger signed SB 777 into law. This new law prohibits any form of bias against homosexuals, bisexuals, transsexuals, cross-dressers, or any other alternative lifestyle choice in California public schools. So thanks to 777 the way is now open to freely persecute the Tyler Harpers of California. Any student who rejects the idea that it is okay for a boy to go to school in a dress, that it is okay for a boy to go the girl's bathroom, that it is okay for the homecoming queen to be male, could quickly find himself in legal hot water. There is only one word for this: insanity. The voters passed Prop 8, and would likely oppose SB 777 if it were put to a statewide popular vote, but the liberal legislators in Sacramento and the liberal judges throughout the state put themselves above the will of the voters. These liberals for some reason see it as their mission to completely undo traditional morality in California through political action and legal coercion.

The only way to undo such laws would be for conservatives to make issues involving sexuality the focal point of their political campaigns—and liberals know that we're not likely to do that. Most conservatives are tolerant people—despite what the liberal media would have you believe—and conservatives are extremely reluctant to define their relationships with other people in terms of sexual orientation. For example, even though I do not consider homosexuality a morally acceptable lifestyle, I have never had any problem working with or befriending people who are homosexual. That seems to me to be the

Christian way. But it is one thing to tolerate and accept, and quite another to have an agenda forced on us by political activists. So while liberals keep advancing their agenda by law, using all the power of the state, conservatives only react to the big picture, as in Prop 8, not to each incremental, and apparently endless, legal chipping away at the Christian morality that used to define American culture.

For a long time, I tried to imagine how these liberals think; why are they so fixated on overturning traditional morality and even our idea of what is normal?

Maggie Gallagher understands them. She writes, "If you really believe that [sexual] orientation is like race, then faithful Catholics, Evangelicals, Mormons, Jews, and Muslims are like racists, and they should be treated by law the same way we treat racists."

And thanks to the Gubernator, that is exactly how the State of California is preparing to treat millions of Christian believers who do not equate race with sexual choice, or interracial marriage with same-sex marriage.

You might think that no one would press the issue to its most extreme conclusions. But this is California. Everything gets pressed to the extremes here. And what happens here happens soon enough in the rest of America.

I confess up front, I'm no expert on politics. I never meant to make myself a political campaigner or an expert on gay marriage or anything remotely similar to that. But when you get put in a box labeled "homophobic" and the media and liberals start throwing rotten vegetables at you, you begin to take an interest in finding out why, in investigating the issues, and in taking a stand in favor of religious freedom and freedom of speech. I was forced to take a stand. I didn't seek out a platform to talk about gay marriage or any other political issues.

To this day, I can't say that politics is my primary interest, or even close to it. I don't want to be a political figure. But just as I did my homework when I prepared for pageant interviews, so I've done it now on the issue that's been shackled to me like a ball and chain; and with the help of the internet, it isn't hard to research.

What did I find? Political correctness and freedom of religion are on a collision course; I was just one roadside accident in a much bigger crash. And it didn't start with Prop 8. In fact, I can't tell you when it started. But I can tell you that the pressure has been building for decades in California. In 1997, for instance, the San Francisco Board of Supervisors voted to require companies that receive city contracts to offer the same benefits to their employees' domestic partners, heterosexual and homosexual, as they do their spouses. In other words, the city demanded that companies downgrade marriage to being no more important than any two people living together who could claim to be domestic partners.

Many firms, from Apple to Charles Schwab, actually already provided these benefits. Many, however, did not. If they had moral objections to doing this, well, apparently that was too bad, the city of San Francisco had decided otherwise. If doing this put a huge financial burden on a company, well that was too bad, too. The only alternative was not to bid for or accept San Francisco city contracts.

But aside from businesses, there were also religious organizations in San Francisco that were put at risk. The Catholic Church has a non-profit subsidiary called Catholic Charities. It received $5.6 million in city contracts to serve 70,000 people, including homeless families, homeless young people, and people with AIDS. The new law on domestic partner benefits was supposed to apply to Catholic Charities just as it applied to Apple. Now the Catholic Church, of course, does not approve of unmarried couples living together, or of homosexual behavior. The city was telling them: So what? They had to provide a subsidy for any employees they had who lived in violation of the teachings of the Catholic Church as a matter of San Francisco law.

I am not a Catholic. But I do know this from my Catholic friends— the Catholic Church would turn the Vatican into a parking garage before it would overturn Catholic teaching. But the city wouldn't back down, either.

Archbishop William J. Levada, leader of the city's 200,000 Catholics at the time, complained to the city that religious organizations "must also be permitted to maintain their operations (including employee benefit plans) in a manner that is consistent with their religious principles. This ensures respect for the constitutional guarantees of free speech and religious freedom."

The mayor at that time, the ever-colorful Willie Brown, told the *San Francisco Examiner*, "I don't think the city should provide any funding with any entity that doesn't comply with city law." He also said: "If Catholic Charities doesn't want to comply, then it should relinquish the funding so that other nonprofits can do their work." In short, Willie Brown was trying to take the place of the pope in dictating the beliefs of the Roman Catholic Church. Either the Church had to compromise its beliefs or it had to cease doing the good work the city had commissioned it to do. In the end, Archbishop Levada came up with a clever compromise: he allowed Church employees to name anyone who lived at home with them to be their beneficiary, which kept the Church from endorsing what it thinks are immoral lifestyles and was good enough for the mayor of San Francisco.

That they reached a compromise was great, but the intrusion of government policy into religious life is only going to get worse if anti-

Christian political correctness keeps gaining ground. In 2009, Joe Solmonese, president of the Human Rights Campaign, a lobbying group for "gay, lesbian, bisexual, and transgender equal rights," was quoted as saying: "When religious organizations step into the public sphere, it should not be surprising to people that they are bound to adhere to the laws in the states that they are operating in." Does that mean that laws can be passed to discriminate against religious beliefs, as in the case of Tyler Harper in Poway?

Maggie Gallagher reviewed the implications of this statement in the pages of *National Review*. She wrote:

> I have been turning these questions over in my mind ever since I became aware of how serious the religious-liberty impact of gay marriage is likely to be. If the negative effects of gay marriage on religious people and institutions are an unintended consequence, why not step forward with generous consequence protections? And if the legal pressures on religious groups are an *intended* consequence, that's something the American people are entitled to know.

Even where you think the positive results of Christian ministry for the public good are unmistakable, liberals are there to try to end the good that's being done.

Chuck Colson is a familiar figure to people of my parent's generation. Involved in the Watergate scandal, he came out of prison a changed man. He dedicated his life to Christ by founding Prison Fellowship to reach prisoners, ex-prisoners, and their families with the transforming love and word of Jesus Christ. He has his work cut out for him. There are 2.3 million people imprisoned in the United States today.

Mark Early of the Justice Fellowship, a related Christian organization, notes that some 400,000 of these 2.3 million will be rearrested within three years. "Why?" he asks. "Because merely warehousing prisoners leaves them unprepared to reenter society as productive citizens. Indeed, it makes them worse."

This recognition led Christian groups to create the InnerChange Freedom Initiative, or IFI, a faith-based program with a proven track record of rehabilitating prisoners. IFI is a purely voluntary association. No prisoner is forced to join. It is also so effective that the state of Iowa funded 40 percent of the program, with the other 60 percent coming from private donors. (If you'd like details on IFI's programs you can visit the IFI website at: *www.ifiprison.org*.) You would think that something as useful and compassionate as this program would be without controversy. And yet a liberal organization, Barry Lynn's Americans United for the Separation of Church and State, sued the state of Iowa, IFI, and Prison Fellowship, claiming that the initiative was unconstitutional. A judge agreed.

He shut down the program and ordered the organizations to repay $1.5 million to the state of Iowa—a heavy burden for a few nonprofits. What is so wrong with the initiative in the eyes of the judge? It is centered around the teachings of Jesus Christ.

The ruling is a faith-buster. Mark Earley of Justice Fellowship says it "could call into question any religious program in state, federal, or local prisons. Merely facilitating a faith-based program could be deemed unconstitutional if this ruling stands."

Early went on to say that the $1.5 million repayment is "unprecedented and sets a troubling precedent. When you combine this legal order with the high legal costs of defending these kinds of suits, the message to faith-based groups is clear: We don't want faith-based groups coming into the public square to offer charitable services."

For liberals, the First Amendment is a one-edged sword. When it comes to protecting the rights of Christians to voice our beliefs, it cuts against us. When it comes to the no-establishment of religion clause of the First Amendment, it cuts against us again. It cuts far beyond anything I am sure George Washington or James Madison ever meant or imagined—so that even offering religion as one path to reform is illegal.

All along the way, as I write this book on my aunt's computer, it continues to strike me as odd that I am doing this before graduating from college. Why should you listen to me? I certainly never thought of myself as intellectually gifted in the way that a political science professor is. I never thought of myself as the spokeswoman for a political cause. I never envisioned myself as having a national audience for my thoughts on freedom of religion. But I know why I do. I think the answer is simple. People listen to me, not, as Donald Trump would have it, because I am pretty. People listen to me because they are too terrified of the political-correctness buzz-saw to speak for themselves; they see me as someone that the liberal media tried to leave behind as road kill. But the media failed, and I speak for those too fearful, too intimidated by political correctness to speak out for themselves.

At one of my last events as Miss California, the jewelers' convention in Las Vegas, many people came up to me to tell me that I am a hero to them. Long lines formed for my autograph. Among them were a bunch of men who were there to provide security (for the jewelry, not me!). These were big, burly men with gunbelts and thick, bullet-proof vests, a SWAT team for security.

While I was signing away, one of them leaned over to me and whispered, "*I am with you.*"

I looked up at him.

"Why are you whispering?"

"Because," he said, "I am in uniform."

So?

I just stared at him. Why do you, a big man armed to the teeth, have to look to a 21-year-old beauty queen to voice your beliefs out loud? Is this what we've come to? Are Americans so cowed by political correctness that we are afraid to voice a reasonable belief? If it is okay for gays come out of the closet, is it necessary for the rest of us to go into one?

Everywhere I went—in the control room of the *Today Show*, on the streets of New York, people would walk up to me to thank me for voicing their opinion. Some are A-list celebrities. One of them has her own highly rated TV show. Why can't they voice their own opinion? Why are they so afraid?

I think back to Donald Trump when he was asked at his press conference what he thought of gay marriage. Even the Donald punted. Even he has to hide with other celebrities and burly SWAT men behind . . . a beauty queen!

Again, I know what they are afraid of. You get attacked as a bigot. You get attacked for behavior you never indulged in but that your attackers certainly did. I don't hate gay people, but I have been attacked in the most hateful manner imaginable. I never use foul language against someone else, yet I am regularly called a "dumb bitch" and a "c**t." I don't go around making threats to gay people, but I have been threatened with my life. I never tried to bully anyone, yet my enemies tried to bully me out of my beliefs. I never said that Keith Lewis or anyone else should be fired because they are gay, yet I lost the crown of Miss California and probably of Miss USA because of who I am, a sincere Evangelical Christian.

As I read the hostile blogs and newspaper columns of my enemies, I get a sense that part of the problem is that many liberals on the other side of this issue get steamed up by what they *imagine* Evangelical Christians like me are thinking or saying behind closed doors.

Here is how one British writer in *The Guardian* imagines what is going on inside my head.

> 'Cuz that's not what God, who was testing her faith by having one of those darn touchy queers ask her the question, wants. The only reason God even *makes* gay people is to test the faith of sweet Christian heterosexuals—he doesn't put them here to live full lives of their own and fall in love and have families and get married. Duh!

As I think I've made clear, those were not my thoughts at all, and to characterize Christian thinking in this way just betrays an ignorance of who Evangelical Christians really are.

In the course of this experience, I've seen many liberals get themselves worked up—not so much about what I said, but about what they assume me to mean. To put it plainly, is standing up for traditional marriage—marriage as our country has always understood it—really the act of a hateful, narrow-minded bigot? Just to say that should show how obviously ridiculous the liberal position is. But that's the way liberals want to slant the debate: all their opponents are bigots.

Over a summer weekend in 2009, protestors came to The Rock, the church I attend, angry about the church's stand on Proposition 8. They waved a rainbow flag, their symbol of diversity. They expected us to either ignore them or confront them with anger. Instead, a group of our people from The Rock came out to hand them water and breakfast bars, and even help the protesters carry their flag to the park near our church. The protestors had one idea of us. I think they were amazed to see who we really are. We are people who, as Christians always say, might hate the sin but love the sinner.

There are gays outside The Rock and gays who are regular worshippers inside The Rock. When it comes to a traditional, Biblically correct view of marriage, Miles will not compromise or water down his belief in what the Bible says: that God created man and woman to be married and be made one. God created sex to be an expression of oneness between a husband and his wife. In my experience, Miles challenges heterosexuals to sexual purity more often than homosexuals, and he believes in sharing his Christian spirit of love and fellowship with all members of the congregation, whatever their state of life. He says that The Rock's membership includes gays—and "we are honored to have them."

Cartoonish ideas of other people often lead to hate and strife. When you come across a living, breathing cartoon like Perez Hilton, it would be easy to give in to disliking everyone who is gay. But I am thankful for all the gay people I've known for keeping me from that.

Just after I was fired, I attended the Ronald Reagan Library in Simi Valley as a guest speaker. After I spoke, two nice, middle-aged women came up to my mom and told her that they thought I was wonderful. They said they were a lesbian couple and that they had been following me and supporting me all along. These are two Americans who understand the principle of free speech. They may not agree with me, but they were just as horrified as anyone else at the hate campaign.

Andrew Sullivan, a famous columnist, blogger, and gay man who advocates for same-sex marriage, had this to say: "Carrie Prejean has had to go through some really bad stuff she didn't deserve, just for inarticulately expressing a valid opinion in front of Perez Hilton."

I hope I wasn't inarticulate. But I am grateful for Mr. Sullivan—who passionately disagrees with me—for seeing my position as "valid." That is the kind of language that builds respect and healing.

I have also heard from an organization called Empowering Spirits Foundation, or ESF, a national lesbian, gay, bisexual, and transgender civil rights organization. They called on everyone "to move forward and cease" condemning me.

"Demeaning Carrie Prejean or others by using terms such as bigot will not advance our cause of civil rights and social justice," they wrote. "The LGBT community must use this period of heightened attention on LGBT issues by engaging others in positive ways," said A. Latham Staples, Empowering Spirits Foundation executive director. "We must not marginalize someone just because they believe differently, as this is the very respect in differing opinion we are asking for from them." Bingo.

They went on to write: "Though ESF strongly disagrees with Prejean's viewpoint regarding same-sex marriage, we believe the hatred expressed by some in the LGBT community for Prejean is unjust. She was asked a question and took the risk to answer it based off of her convictions, knowing that her answer would be scrutinized.

While ESF disagrees with her opinion, she had every right to answer the question based on how she felt."

I appreciate that so much! That, it seems to me, is the sort of freedom of speech, and tolerance, that my grandfather risked his life to defend when he fought at the Battle of the Bulge; that is the American way.

CHAPTER ELEVEN

Stand Up for Yourself

Letters have been coming to me by the yard since I made my first *Today Show* appearance.

One letter I received was from a father about his little girl, Emily. It has stuck with me.

> When she was born the nurses said, "Oh, she is a beautiful baby!" Well, we know that in truth most babies when they are first born—they are not the prettiest to behold. But the nurses assured us—"no, we're serious; we see a lot of babies; and she is really beautiful." Of course, we are just happy as all get out to be first-time parents, so we really didn't think too much about it!

As Emily grew into a baby, and toddler, and little girl, my wife when going out with her into public to go to the grocery store, etc., would constantly have strangers come up to her and tell her how beautiful her daughter was. After a while, with all this unsolicited attention, we realized that perhaps there was something to all of the comments and attention. Where I am going with all this, is that as a father this started to create serious concern within me. Here was my little girl that to the world she was outwardly very pleasing, very beautiful. My mind went into protection mode. And as I prayed and thought about this, I realized that her protection began within herself.

So ever since she was about 2 years old, I have had a saying with my daughter..."Which is more important: pretty on the inside? Or pretty on the outside?" And I have ingrained pretty on the inside, explaining that a person cannot be truly beautiful unless they are pretty on the inside, and that means that they have Christ in their heart. Emily has the outward beauty thing down. I wanted to do what I could as a father to ground her inner values. She has since asked Christ into her heart, praying with her mother when she was six to enter that most sacred relationship with our Lord.

He goes on to write . . .

When Emily was around four or five years old, I was driving her to pre-school, and was talking about pretty on the inside again. At that time, the incident with Paris Hilton landing in trouble and going to jail hit the news. And I explained to my little girl that here was Paris, a very beautiful woman with lots of things going for her. And yet she had some very bad habits and made some very bad choices. Of course, people can change, and it may be so for Paris. Yet for purposes of illustration, Paris became the example of someone who was *not* pretty on the inside.

Carrie, I write because I am thankful to find the example of a beautiful lady who IS pretty on the inside. There are a lot of beautiful girls out there. They need role models to know that it can be a wonderful thing and a God-given blessing to be made beautiful, a woman who is also capable, confident, smart, and courageous. Thank you for being true to God's leading and being true to who He has made you to be.

This father suggested—and I blush at the suggestion—that I am a role model who should give advice to girls. Well, I have always tried to be a role model. And I do know that I have learned a lot through experience, and there is nothing I would like more than to help young girls avoid the many pitfalls that can await them out there in the world, to do what they can to cultivate *inner* beauty, the beauty that matters most. It's so unfortunate that the only models so many girls today have of what a young woman should be are pop icons like Miley Cyrus, who are anything but moral examples.

So let me try to present the right kind of example with this chapter. I won't do it—in fact, I can't do it—from a pedestal of imaged perfection. But I can do it as someone who strives to live the right way, as someone who has been tested in a public trial by fire, and as a young woman who has struggled hard against challenges that many other young women will face. I hope I can offer some useful lessons, lessons grounded in what faith and experience have taught me. A crisis has a way of sharpening perception, and I think in the wake of the controversy that engulfed me, that seized a crown from my head, ripped a sash from my shoulder, and put my character on trial (after a frenzy of mudslinging), that eight lessons stand as signposts—signposts that I want to guide my own path in the future, and that others might find helpful, too.

First, be true to yourself—don't let anyone browbeat you, bully you, or trick you into doing something that you feel uncomfortable doing.

I doubt that there has ever been a time or place in which young women have had to grow up with so much coarseness heaped on us—not by young men, not by enemies from another country, but by our elders. To put it bluntly, we are forced to find our way into womanhood in a brutally sexualized world. The movies, TV, and the internet ooze with sexual come-ons that are utterly divorced from what sex is really all about: the love between a husband and wife, and the children that love produces. Unfortunately, pornography has become mainstreamed—it rushes at us through big screens, little screens, portable screens; soft-core porn is on mainstream TV cable stations, hard-core porn is just a mouse click away on the internet, and the envelope of what is acceptable seems to get pushed farther and farther as more and more people are exposed to this material.

The result is that girls grow up in a culture where it is hard to have an innocent, healthy, normal view of themselves, how they should behave, how they should act, and how they should dress. From at least the age of thirteen, the fashion sense of girls is led by a super-sexualized image of what a young lady should look like. Take Abercrombie & Fitch, a teen clothing store that rakes in profits by selling sex (in all forms) to kids. Girls in particular are vulnerable to the image stores like this try to sell them of what's "cool" or "sexy." This store—and others like it—grab Mommy and Daddy by the wallet and won't let go. Parents find themselves unwilling to call a stop to this madness, perhaps because they might be caught up in it themselves—they are as vulnerable to media manipulation as anyone else.

Kids are under peer pressure, sure, but it is parents who are, well, the parents—and too many parents seem unwilling to take the time and make the effort and set the standards and *live* the standards that parenthood requires. More important than peer pressure, kids model their behavior on that of their elders. Before kids even have peers, they're looking and watching and learning from what Mom and Dad do. It doesn't help if what Mom and Dad do is put Mary or Susie in front of the TV all day. I don't know about you, but I don't want Hollywood raising my kids. Considering what I have seen of the Hollywood crowd and what they show us, it doesn't surprise me that so many girls think that "girls-gone-wild" behavior is how every girl is expected to act on Spring Break. All the moral guardrails that parents and schools used to put up to protect young women have been torn down. That might be useful to the sleaze merchants who peddle DVDs of girls getting drunk and lifting their shirts, but it's certainly not helpful to teenage and college age girls.

How can we defend this? It seems to me we can't. It seems to me that before we let our daughters make their way in this world, they need to be given the shield of faith, a moral education that is worlds removed from the values of Hollywood, a moral education that is based on timeless truth—however hard some of that truth might seem. They need to know that mistakes can haunt them forever. What I most want Emily and other young girls to know is that they should live every day as if everything they do might become public knowledge; they should know too that God is watching their every step.

Today, it's not just morality that we need, but we need to guard our privacy. With the internet, too many young people are laying themselves open to the world in ways that might not be in their best interests. A snapshot of anything a girl does can be seen by everyone she knows—and can even be seen by many she doesn't. A snapshot has only to be posted on the internet, and it will live forever.

Believe me, I know.

After the old photos of me came out, Miles began to hear from concerned people inside The Rock. They asked, "Will Carrie's pictures hurt the image of the Church?" Some wondered if it might be best to put a little distance between The Rock and me. Miles's answer was firm. He said, "People have a perception that if you are imperfect you don't have the right to have an opinion. If that's the case, then no one would have opinions." He also smiles when we talk about this. "It's a good thing," Miles says, "that most people don't have pictures of what all of us were doing when we were seventeen." It's basic Christian doctrine that we're all sinners in need of forgiveness. We just have to ask for it, and we need to be willing to give it.

I appreciate Miles's support. But every time I read in the papers about some promiscuous teen, it brings home to me just how damaging a frivolous or thoughtless moment can be. It also brought home to me how important it is for young women to stand our ground and learn to say, "No."

This worried me so much, that I decided to set an example by blogging an apology.

To all my fans out there:

To the ones who have supported me since day one, and to the thousands of little girls who look up to me as a role model, let me apologize for old pictures you may have seen of me. I acknowledge that I should never have put myself in a position where a photographer could snap inappropriate images of me and sell them for a lot of money. I was a model at the time, and very naïve. I should have known better. Again, I am sorry. There is an important lesson here for all young women who are coming of age in this highly sexualized world. We are all children of God. Our bodies are temples of the Lord. We should earn respect and admiration for our hearts, not for showing skin to try to look sexy. I hope you learn from my mistakes. After all, in your life you too will be faced with similar decisions. Never do things to seek man's approval. Do things to seek God's approval. Listen to that still quiet voice. In my case, I didn't feel right about this photo shoot. I knew something just wasn't right when the photographer showed me what I was going to be wearing. I should have taken a stand. I have since learned that your outer beauty can only get you so far in life. At the end of your life, you are only left with one thing—your soul, what's inside it, and the wisdom from God to choose right from wrong.

Sincerely,

Carrie

I want to tell girls that you don't have to be another public spectacle in the sexual marketplace. If you have an internal filter in your heart and mind, like Emily's dad is teaching her to have, you can filter out all the peer pressure. It's not about do's and don'ts, it about what you really want for yourself. To teens: You don't have to just go out and drink because everybody else is doing it. Go to a party some time and just watch while everyone else is drinking and you're not. See how they behave. Is that what you want to be—red-faced, out-of-control, or worse? There's a lot more to life than that; it's a better life to keep all your senses, including your mind, intact, unpolluted by alcohol or drugs, and appreciating God's creation—from a beautiful sunset to a beautiful person—as someone who is beautiful inside and out.

One other thing—you can be athletic and feminine at the same time. God gave us our bodies, and it's perfectly right that we use them in ways where we can give glory to God by making our bodies, our temples of the Holy Spirit, strong and fast. You can do all that and still be a girl. You can play basketball, tennis, soccer, volleyball, or be a football cheerleader. You can get out there and sprint around like the best running back in the NFL and still be the girl you've always been. You can do all that, and still be pretty on the inside. Just remember to whom you owe the glory; just remember that even if you fail, even if you come in last place, if you did the best you could, if you gave God your best effort, you did just fine. I'm a competitor, but I know that it's not just the winner who merits God's love.

Two: Never fear that God's standard is the right standard.

Often in my life, I've seen people succumb to the peer pressure to do the wrong thing, to think, for instance, that hooking up and promiscuity are no big deal. I've seen how girls are pressured into thinking that unless they're willing to sleep around, they won't be able to "get a boyfriend." I know how easy it is to think, perversely, that to be good is bad ("she's a prude," or a "goody-goody"), and to be a bad girl is good.

But the "hook-up" culture only opens people up to a whole lot of unnecessary pain. At the most basic level, of course, casual sex leads to horrible, sometimes deadly, diseases. But it goes deeper than that. Sleeping around is psychologically and spiritually damaging, especially to girls. It leads to loneliness and destroys a woman's sense of self worth. After all, casual sex isn't about love at all, and it does not lead to commitment. Girls who fall into this lifestyle (and I've seen so many girls who have) don't even know what love is. In fact, they do not believe that they are worthy of love.

Don't let the whole "beauty queen" thing fool you. True love and commitment are not about how pretty or sexy a girl is. Men might like to look at me, they might think of me as sexy, but that isn't love. It's hard for a man to appreciate a woman's heart, when today's culture places so much emphasis on outer beauty and how "hot" a girl is. Believe me, I've had my fair share of heartbreaks. I know as well as the next girl how much it hurts to find out that your boyfriend has cheated on you. Maybe you caught him lying, or you just don't feel secure in a relationship. And I know what a broken heart feels like.

Another thing I've learned: never feel that your standards are too high. A girl should have ideals, and she should expect the man she's with to live up to them—or at least to try. Of course, it cuts both ways. A woman should strive to be worthy of the man she dreams of. Before you focus on being in a relationship with someone else, set your sights on developing yourself as the woman God made you to be. Be independent. When you have that focus, everything else just falls into place. Sometimes if you just stop looking, the right man will run right into you.

Our culture nowadays equates love with sex. The word "love" gets thrown around so casually that people don't even know what it means. We look to pop culture to define the term for us. (After all, Miley Cyrus can sing about love—she *must* know what it is.) Or how about those songs on the radio kids hear on a daily basis, touting promiscuity and the supposed joys of "making love." After all, I doubt any of these singers even know what true love means. All the pop culture knows is that love definitely should include a lot of sex.

I encourage girls to rise above that worldly standard. The lifestyle the world encourages us to embrace only leads to misery; it can't lead to love. True love is about commitment. It goes so much deeper than any kind of physical closeness, or the way someone makes you feel, and it certainly cannot be found in a one-night stand.

Three: Grace turns losses into gains and accidents into your best opportunities.

The amazing thing about grace is that once you seek it, it will not only help you avoid making the wrong choices—it will lead you to opportunities that are far better and more satisfying than anything you ever imagined.

When I was at the center of a hate campaign, it seemed as if my whole world was coming apart. That plane ride from Las Vegas to New York was the loneliest ride I've ever had. I silently prayed and prayed, and yet felt God was not with me. If we sometimes feel abandoned like I did, it's not because God isn't listening. It is because we're impatient. As soon as I landed, spiritual guidance was already there, waiting for me, just a few blocks from my hotel.

I think back to the night I was given the wrong directions to the event at the children's hospital. Had I been given the right directions,

I would have driven several more hours to sit among a throng of people at a rubber-chicken dinner. It didn't work out that way. At first, when I got to the hospital, I came in from the parking lot with my sash and gown. Standing there under fluorescent lights, I felt foolish and out of place. But that very mistake took me just where I needed to be: the children's cancer ward.

God keeps teaching us that what we want is not what we need; and what we get fills both our needs and our wants. I know, it is difficult to let go of what you really want. Miles saw years of hard work on the gridiron come to a complete end in the NFL. He had to run into that brick wall before he could see where God needed him to be.

The challenges we run into can seem rude, abrupt, like the end of the world. Miles wanted a big, glittering Super Bowl ring. I wanted the glittering crown of Miss USA, or even Miss Universe. When we learn to toss away our fondest ambitions as trash—we find a crown awaiting us that is far more meaningful and beautiful than anything we could ever imagine for ourselves.

Life will distract you with drama. "Don't care about all the drama," Miles says. "God has a plan for you. Don't get distracted from his plan."

Four: Seek advice from a "multitude of counsel."

People come up to me all the time and tell me that they would have crumbled under the pressure I was under. What they don't realize is that I did crumble. I was knitted back together thanks to the support I had from strong people around me.

The Book of Proverbs advises us to seek "a multitude of counsel." I had a multitude, from my mom and dad, my sister, my pastor, my friends, and my supporters. I had a lot of people to turn to and to remind me that I was on the right path, to show me that people were with me and behind me. When you face your trials, having friends, family, and a faith community that shares your commitment is the only way to make it through.

Miles says that the effort to stay true to our faith is a lifelong struggle. "This is a fight between Mike Tyson and Evander Holyfield," Miles says, "and you are going to get hit—and you might even get your ear bitten off."

As the Book of Timothy promises, if you're a Christian, you are going to be persecuted. You are going to be made fun of. You are going to be called names. Your commitment to Christ is going to alienate people you'd like to have as friends.

Whenever this path seems like a tall order, I try to remember how easy we have it today compared to the earliest Christians, the ones who suffered torture and death rather than renounce Christ. If they could be so brave, can't we stand together to shuck off a little social embarrassment and ostracism? When you are given an opportunity to stand up for Christ, do it. No questions asked. Don't compromise your faith for anyone or anything.

Five: Forgiveness heals.

At Liberty University, I thanked Perez Hilton for giving me this chance to proclaim my beliefs as a Christian. I was pushed hard. In these pages I have pushed back. I think it is all right and more than a little natural to get angry and set the record straight. But I've learned not to let anger make a home in my heart. After all, I was accused of being a hater. The challenge to me is not to hate anyone. And so I struggle to love everyone who has crossed me, as I hope they forgive any slights or injuries I might have inflicted on them. There are few wiser words than those of the Lord's Prayer: "Forgive us our trespasses as we forgive those who trespass against us."

Six: Don't leave yourself outside of the circle of forgiveness.

You are going to make mistakes. You are going to do things that you are not especially proud of. Realize that, acknowledge that, *change* that, but don't harp on it.

Christians are often accused of being judgmental people. But we, more than anyone else, know how little excuse we have for judging anyone else. We are not perfect people. We are imperfect people trying to uphold a perfect standard.

"The Church doesn't exist to house perfect people," Miles says. "It exists to help people walk away from where they are. It exists to help them be more obedient."

Seven: Don't let the culture convince you that trying to hold to a high standard is being "too judgmental."

The Rock has a lot of regular families and married couples with children. But we also have strippers and even active call girls in our Church. The fact that they are in the pews is their acknowledgement that they want to change. Miles likens their lifestyle to that of an alcoholic. One person wants with all her heart and soul to get out and live a cleaner life—and does it. Another person wants to try to have it both ways, to keep going to Church while staying in a trap of addiction and sin.

"You love both of them," Miles says, "but you've got to keep moving forward."

It is the high standard set by Christ that attracts Christians to the Church, but it is also what infuriates others. "People object to the standards of God's love," Miles says. "But it is not my standard!"

If people are offended by your belief in God's standards, that is truly their problem, not yours. One such standard is the Biblical teaching that marriage is between a man and a woman. But holding such a standard is not the same thing as being intolerant. It would surprise many in Hollywood to see how everyone who comes to The Rock is met with love, encouragement, and acceptance. After all, the splinter in your eye may be nothing compared to the redwood log in mine. Judgment of people (as opposed to behavior) is just seen as another sin.

Miles laughs and says, "People in this Church are beauty contestants, criminals, lawyers, doctors, crackheads. . . . So wonderful to have all these people in this Church. All servants of one. I am honored beyond belief that they feel loved and accepted at The Rock."

Eight: Stand up with courage.

This last point comes home to me through the story of another beauty queen, another one who stood up on a stage to risk her very life. I am so grateful to Miles for making me aware of the lessons of the Book of Esther and helping our whole congregation draw strength from it.

The story of Esther takes place in ancient Persia, where the Jews were a captive people under the rule of the Persian king Ahasuerus. After the king's wife refuses to display her beauty before the guests at a feast, he removes her. (I guess I'm not the first beauty queen to be fired.)

Having gotten rid of his queen, King Ahasuerus has to shop for a replacement. So he orders his court to present him with the most beautiful girls in his kingdom. A kind of personal beauty pageant is held for him. The girls are brought before him one at a time, and the king chooses the most beautiful and desirable girl, Esther.

But Esther has a secret. She is a Jewess. Not only that, she is related to one of the king's top advisors, Mordechai, a loyal subject who uncovers and stops an assassination plot against the king. The king, however, has no knowledge of Mordechai's usefulness. Instead, at the king's right hand is a jealous man, Haman, appointed to be the king's prime minister. It doesn't take Haman long to start to look for ways to get rid of Mordechai once and for all.

Haman demands that Mordechai bow down before him. The Jewish advisor refuses and falls into disfavor. While Mordechai sits in exile outside the palace gates, Haman plans to convince the king that the Jews of Persia are a threat. He knows that if he can get the king to kill all the Jews—to commit genocide—Haman can eradicate Mordechai along with all his people. In time, Haman orders a special gallows constructed just for Mordechai.

Using manipulative language, Haman manages to convince the king to sign the edict, not revealing the massive scale of the genocide that will result from this order. On a certain date, all the Jews of Persia will be put to the sword.

Suddenly, the fate of her whole people falls into Esther's lap. She knows that if she steps out of line in any way, the king will get rid of her, too. If she reveals herself as Jewish, she will suffer the same fate as her relatives.

Esther asks all Jews in Persia to fast and pray with her, as she tries to discern what to do. When you ask God to direct you, He will. And so an answer comes to Esther. She is led to seek an audience with the king. This is a very bold and dangerous move for a woman, even for a queen. To initiate an audience with the king of Persia, a man who holds the power of life and death, takes courage. Unless the king holds out his golden scepter—showing that he agrees that her interruption of his time is necessary—the intruder, even a queen, will be put to death.

Esther risks death and boldly places herself in the king's presence. She takes the occasion to invite the king and Haman to a series of feasts. The king accepts. What happens next is a coincidence, which in this case, as in so many, can only be attributed to divine intervention. One night, the king is lying awake, unable to get a wink of sleep. To help him drift off, he asks his attendants to read him the court records. (Sounds better than a sleeping pill.) By chance, one record tells of how Mordechai saved the king from assassins. The records make it clear that Mordechai's act of loyalty was never acknowledged, much less rewarded.

When Haman next stands before the king, Ahasuerus tells his prime minister that there is a man he wants to honor above all other subjects. How best to honor him?

Haman, believing this honor to be for himself, says that the man should be robed in the king's royal clothes and led around on the king's horse.

The king agrees. Then he orders Haman—to his surprise and horror—to honor Mordechai in this way.

Now that the king is becoming aware of what is going on around him, Esther takes the opportunity at the next banquet to tell him the rest. She divulges that she is Jewish. She reveals that Haman has plotted the annihilation of all Jews, including his queen and his new hero, Mordechai.

The upshot is that Esther and her people are saved, Mordechai rises in the king's court, and Haman goes to the gallows that he had prepared for his enemy.

That's the story, retold over the centuries during the Jewish Purim festivals. In the Christian tradition, it is often overlooked. After my story broke, Miles invited me to a warm and lengthy discussion before the congregation. He drew out some of the lessons from Esther. He said that we should all look to her as an example of strength and character. As Miles says, she shows us how to S.T.A.N.D. for our faith.

The "S" is for "Stare-down courage." Esther asks for the Jews in the capital to pray and fast—and she will join them. She then risks death to stand before the king. If we are to stand up for our beliefs, we must be willing to stare intimidation in the face and say, "I am going to do what's right."

The "T" is for "Trust in the truth."

We should live according to the truth of God's Word alone.

My critics have often pointed out that if I had only answered Perez Hilton's question differently, I could have had the crown. Maybe I could have, but it wouldn't have been a truthful answer—true to what I believe and true to who I am, and that is more important to me than any crown.

The "A" is for "Accept God's sovereign provision."

When we are faced with tough challenges, God himself provides for us. God provided my pastor in my darkest hour, at a time when I felt utterly alone and afraid.

The "N" is for "Never fear man over God."

Esther walked into the king's presence not knowing if he would lower his scepter or not. She had every reason to tremble before the king, but she knew that her duty to God was greater. People will always attack you. But as long as you stick by the truth—as long as you are right by God—you have integrity. There is a kind of safety in this: "For if God is for us, who can be against us?" (Romans 8:28–31.) God has a bigger crown than any man can give us. God's approval is the only approval that matters.

And the "D"? It stands for "Die to self."

When she faces the likely outcome of her impertinence in asking for an audience with the king, Esther resigns herself to her course of action and says, "And if I perish, I perish."

Win, lose, or draw, she is sticking with God.

Miles writes: "Your life is not about you and doesn't belong to you. God has a plan that is bigger than you. You're not here to save your life, but to give it as Jesus did. Just as Carrie was faced with an opportunity to stand up for her faith, each one of us has opportunities to stand up for God as well—at work, in our communities, etc. We must remember, just as Carrie found out, that no experience is so bad that God can't use it to make an impact for His kingdom."

Miles goes on to say: "Take a stand for what you believe. Don't be afraid to stand up for the truth. God entrusted people like you and me with his Gospel. We are the ones who must carry it out!"

We all have gifts. I am still learning how God wants me to use my gifts. I am finding out to my astonishment that my misfortune is opening up opportunities I never believed I would have. I am sure that with those opportunities will come fresh temptations and dangers to avoid.

You, too, have gifts—the gifts of love that only you can offer. You, too, will be tempted to get off course, to please a boyfriend, a photographer, a producer, a boss, rather than do what you think is right.

To help you stand firm, God reveals himself and his plans to us through prayer, his word, the counsel of godly people, and the seeming miracles and divine appointments of life. There will be times when you pray and the Holy Spirit will clearly direct you one way or another. Some things that you think are not important you will be directed to see as very important. And there will be times when you anguish over something and God will say, "This is no big deal." This has happened to me, and in every instance, after a little while, I realize that the still, quiet voice was right.

How do you know when you are in communication with God? You will know. God is consistent. His truth is not going to change.

There may be times God will tell you, "Do this"—but it will not be clear why. It may not make sense at the time, but you can be assured that you are being led in the right way. There will be times when you will feel alone, and that still, quiet voice will be your best friend. He will always be your best friend.

I'm done with this story. All this stuff, from Las Vegas to the studios of New York—all this *drama*—is not real to me anymore; it belongs to a different life. In a sense, it never was real; it was a world of superficial values; values that are broadcast to us every day, but that are merely passing fancies, that do not reflect the honest truth about our lives, their purpose, and how we should conduct ourselves in the light of eternity. What is real is the love of God and how we express that love when we're tempted, discouraged, or challenged.

Keep your eye on the prize, for the only crown that truly glitters is the one you get to keep forever.

Acknowledgments

To God: Thank you for giving me a final chance to honor you in front of the entire world. Thank you for trusting me with this large task. I am honored to have endured it. I am forever grateful for the sacrifice you made for me. I give all the glory and honor to you.

To Mom: You are a wonderful woman, beautiful inside and out. Thank you for bathing, clothing, listening, teaching, mentoring, guiding, loving me. I will always remember your sacrifice as a mother, thank you for staying home all those years and instilling in me the values I will remember forever.

To Dad: Thank you, dad, for teaching me to be proud of being a young conservative woman. You have given me so much, and I can't thank you enough. You have given up so much, for Chrissy, Billy, and me. I am so blessed for the close relationship we have had over the years. I will always be daddy's little girl.

To Sis: My best friend. We're practically twins! I can't begin to tell you how much I appreciate you, not only for your service in the military, but for teaching me so much about life. You have taught me, we can agree to disagree. Love you, sis.

To Billy: My big brother. Even though we are seven years apart, I still look up to you and admire your independence. Thank you for teaching me to dream big. You have accomplished so much from such a small dream as a little boy.

To my nieces Ally Faith and Hailey Jane: I love you girls so much. I hope you have learned through this, to always stand up for what's right. Your Auntie Carrie loves you so much. Can't wait to see you again someday.

To my Kyle: I am so blessed to have you in my life. You have shown me what love is. Thank you for supporting me through all this drama. I knew when we met there was something so special about you. I can't wait to see where the Lord leads us in our future.

Pastor Miles: I wouldn't be still standing had it not been for you. You and Debbie have been there for me when no one else was around. Thank you for being my pastor, my friend, and a part of the family. Your guidance and council have meant so much to me.

Pam and Debbie: Thank you for teaching me everything I know about pageants. Had it not been for your love and guidance, I would not be where I am at today. Everyone at the Miss Greater San Diego pageant, thank you for molding me to be a strong woman.

To my family at Regnery Publishing—Tom, Marji, Mark, Jeff, and Harry—Thank you for allowing me to tell my story. Thank you all for your brilliant ideas! You all have helped so much with my book, I couldn't have done it with out you. Thank you for the many hours spent editing, fixing, revising this book. I'm so grateful for the wonderful team of yours. I am so excited about *Still Standing*. I know this book will be a success for us all. I want you all to know how much I appreciate the time and energy you have spent making it nothing short of a bestseller. Every single one of you has added something special to it. I look forward to working with you again.

Mary Beth—Thank you for the many hours we have spent on the phone going over edits, making sure everything is right on! I've appreciated your input and advice along the way.

Kathleen and Sally—I'm so excited for my book tour with you ladies. Thank you for being such a great marketing team.

To Charles LiMandri: I can't thank you enough. You have not only been my lawyer, but my friend. Thank you for your detailed edits and ideas for *Still Standing*.

To Larry Ross, Keri, and Melany: Thank you for taking the time to make edits to my book. I'm so glad we were able to get your input as well as accurate information needed.

To my family, friends, and fans: Thank you for forever believing me, supporting me, and enduring with me. This book would not be a success had it not been for everyone who contributed to it.

Peace, Love, and Respect,

Sincerely,

Carrie Prejean

Index